Betsy and Saganaga: One Life, One Lake

For Betsy–

I thank you for the time we have spent together and for trusting me with your stories.

–Carol

10 9 8 7 6 5 4 3 2

Copyright 2004
Adventure Publications, Inc.
820 Cleveland St. S
Cambridge, MN 55008
800-678-7006
www.adventurepublications.net
All rights reserved.
Printed in U.S.A.
ISBN-13: 978-1-59193-093-8
ISBN-10: 1-59193-093-6

Table of Contents

Sidebars:

From *The Singing Wilderness*

"Until the day when I discovered it, my life had been dominated by the search for a perfect wilderness lake. Always before me was the ideal, a place not only remote, not only of great beauty, but possessed of an intangible quality and spirit that typified to me all of the unbroken north beyond all roads. Time and again I thought I had found it, but always there was something wrong, some vague, unreasoned lack of shape or size, some totally unexplainable aspect involved with the threat of accessibility. Above all, I wanted vistas that controlled not only moonrises and sunsets, but the northern lights and the white mists of the river mouths at dawn. Sometimes it was a matter of intuition and feeling, an unsettled state of mind more than any particular physical character, that made me push on. The search drew me farther and farther into the bush, and I finally began to wonder if I actually knew what I was looking for and if I would know when I had found it.

Then one golden day I came to Saganaga. My first glimpse from the western narrows was enough, and as I stood there and looked out across the broad blue reaches to the east with their fleets of rocky islands, the hazy blue hills toward the hinterlands of the Northern Light Country, I knew I had reached my goal. How I knew without having explored the lake, I cannot say, but the instant I saw the lake, I realized it was the end of my search, and that there was nothing more beyond the hills. I shall never forget the sense of peace and joy which was mine at the discovery. Perhaps I was ready for Saganaga; perhaps all the searching that had gone before had prepared me. Whatever it was, I was content at last, knowing that I would find in the lonely solitude the realization of all my dreams." [Sigurd Olson, The Singing Wilderness. (1956; reprinted Minneapolis: University of Minnesota Press, 1997)]

A Note from Carol DeSain

Betsy and I met in 1992. It was early in November when I was helping Tom Eckel, a local commercial fisherman, put in a temporary dock at Betsy's place. We used the dock to load nets and fish boxes in the morning and unload whitefish after dark every day until the lake froze. Betsy would wander down to visit with us when we arrived and Tom would share his fish with her. I was curious about this woman with the bright blue eyes who lived on Saganaga Lake at the end of the Gunflint Trail, but I did not come back to visit for several years. Finally, one November, I came back alone. I wasn't sure she would welcome a stranger, but I took a chance.

However, my introduction to Saganaga Lake was years earlier as a young woman eager to paddle these waters and venture into the wilderness. Saganaga Lake was a jumping-off point, one lake on a long list of interconnected waterways, a lake of passage that I needed to paddle across to achieve another destination on a blue and yellow map. Every trip across Sag left a memorable impression. Sometimes I was calmed by its geography, sometimes captivated by what I learned about myself when I was there, but always haunted by the experience. I was a visitor then, I still am, but I know more now. Saganaga Lake is now my destination. I keep coming back again and again to learn about whitefish and otters in November from Tom Eckel, and to learn about those who lived along this shore-line from Betsy.

I am now anchored to this landscape. In this geography I am sustained and connected hand-by-hand to those who have cared for this land long before I arrived. It is a simple gift of relationship. Like Betsy, I have found a place where I belong. She has reminded me that I am connected to the land intimately through other people. Without their stories, my own stories lose context. Without human connections, I am always a visitor who is never at home.

— Carol DeSain

Carol visited Betsy on numerous occasions and this book is adapted from the manuscript she submitted based on those interviews.

Introduction

This is the story about a relationship between a woman and a lake. It is a story about a love that has survived great poverty, a world war, fires, wind, loneliness and time. The border between the United States and Canada cuts through Saganaga Lake, and this woman, even in her 80s, continued to live in this wilderness. She has lived in this landscape since she was an 18-year-old girl, watching the sun rise each morning and fade in the evening on Raven's Rock across the bay.

The lake itself is large and spectacular, remote even by today's standards. Its history suggests that it has always been a place beyond the end of the road. Over the years, the few who settled here traveled to this place along rivers and lakes and settled in places where food was plentiful and transportation not too difficult. These practical considerations were always tempered by the sheer beauty of the place.

The islands of Saganaga leave a visual impression that haunts the memory. In perfect harmony, white pines grow from rock and water and light. They stand here as sentinels of the centuries, whispering stories into the wind, casting silhouettes in the moonlight. It has taken hundreds of thousands of years to create this scene. It is a gift.

Raven's Rock on Saganaga Lake

Some of the oldest rocks on the planet are found here, pressed beneath Saganaga granite. This is the tablet over which glaciers retreated four times, gouging the rocks in ways that almost seem like messages from the past. The trees of Saganaga Lake are a virgin forest, red and white pines mixed with spruce, tamarack, cedar, birch and balsam. Their seeds feed mice, chipmunks, grosbeaks and white-throated sparrows. Brown bears browse for berries and grubs in the forest. The tree canopy shields snowshoe hares, white-tailed deer, porcupines and moose. These creatures, in turn, attract wolves, foxes, fishers, lynx and owls to the forest.

The waters of Saganaga Lake are clear and deep, flowing from the Granite and Seagull rivers and Northern Light and Ottertrack lakes to create a 20,000-acre sanctuary. These waters are home to trout, whitefish, herring and pike. Beaver, mink, muskrat and otters live along the shore. And mergansers, kingfishers and loons dive below the lake's surface to feed.

There were Ojibwe Indians here as the French voyageurs passed through from the late 1700s to the mid-1800s, transporting furs to the East. Other Europeans began arriving in the area in the late 1800s, first as trappers, later working in the logging camps of northern Wisconsin and Minnesota. Some decided to stay to live off the land, but the ones who thrived were those who truly learned the ways of the wilderness.

Residents of Saganaga Lake are almost gone now. The few that remain are, like Betsy, a bit ornery, unimpressed by the modern age and its tourists. When they are gone we may have seen the last of a breed of hard-working, self-sufficient, self-reliant people. Each of them has a story to tell, and when they go, we lose their stories.

This is Betsy Powell's story. It is only one story, but it is also one of the last.

The woman with the bright blue eyes, Betsy Powell

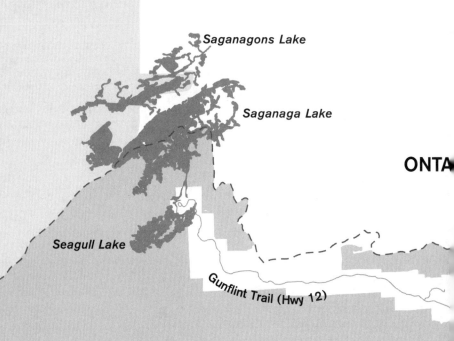

QUETICO
PROVINCIAL PARK

Saganagons Lake

Saganaga Lake

ONTA

Seagull Lake

Gunflint Trail (Hwy 12)

BOUNDARY WATERS
CANOE AREA WILDERNESS

MINNESOTA

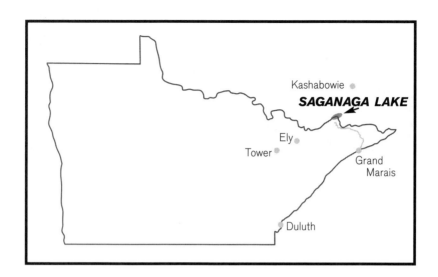

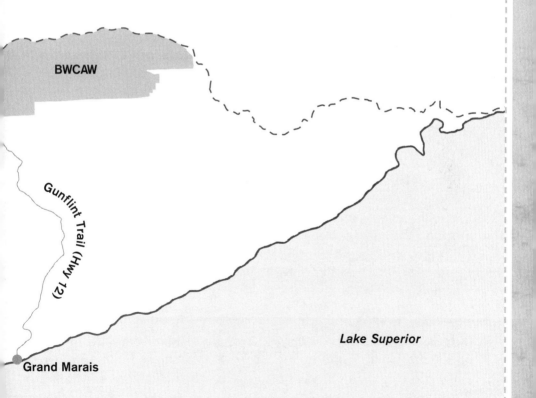

Kashabowie

SAGANAGA LAKE

Ely

Tower

Grand Marais

Duluth

BWCAW

Gunflint Trail (Hwy 12)

Lake Superior

Grand Marais

Chapter 1

Bruneau Family Beginnings

Once in a while a man or a woman comes into the world in the wrong time or the wrong place. They are raised in loving households, educated, cared for, taught the skills that are expected to support them and judged by the standards of the family. But they are different. They are possessed by a yearning that cannot be tamed or altered. These individuals are not simply motivated by the circumstances of their lives, they are inspired. Sooner or later they find a way to escape and they find a place to live where their differences are meaningful or useful. It may take years or it may simply take a helping hand.

Betsy Bruneau was one of these different ones. She was born to Rosmyn and Louise Bruneau in Tower, Minnesota on November 25, 1920. Differences, however, are hardly noticed when you are the seventh of 10 children—four older sisters, two older brothers, two younger sisters and a younger brother—in a family caught in the poverty and uncertainty of the 1930s. The priorities of the household were simple: find enough work to raise the children and feed the family and provide a tithe to the Mormon Church. Pa had worked at a local brewery until 1920, when Prohibition cost him his job. Then, with seven children to feed, he went to work at Olson's General Store in Tower. From his $75 monthly pay, Pa faithfully gave $7.50 to the Mormon Church.

Like most families of the 1920s and 1930s, the Bruneaus lived a very simple life. Ma, Pa and the ten children lived in a two-bedroom house in Tower. Pa left the house at 6 a.m. for work at Olson's. Ma tended to the children and household and ran a busy laundry business from home servicing the local and summer residents on Lake Vermillion. Pa was usually back home by 6 p.m., often with leftover food from the store.

The Bruneau family: Top row from left: Charlotte, Alice, Virginia.
Middle row: Dorothy, Rosmyn, Louise, Rosmyn Jr.
Front row: Betsy, Marge, George.

Daily chores for the children included helping Ma with the laundry. She needed a great deal of water and the only source was the town's river, the East Two. The children were expected to haul the water up the hill from the river. This was a never-ending chore that required loading a large copper boiler onto a wagon, pulling it carefully down the steep hill to the river, then filling it up, one tin pitcher at a time by crawling up and down the riverbank many times. Then, they would haul the wagon back up the hill with about ten gallons of water. This was hard work; water was needed every day and it usually took three to four young Bruneaus to get the wagon back uphill. This chore was made even more challenging in winter when the river froze, as the children first had to chop an opening in the ice with an axe to get to the water. After filling the boiler, they would push and pull it on a sleigh up the steep hill to get home.

Summers were the busiest times for laundry. Every day, Pa would collect the dirty laundry from Arnsen's launch, the boat that ran mail and supplies to the cabin owners on Lake Vermillion. Pa was already supplying cabin owners with groceries from Olson's store where he worked, so he picked up and delivered laundry as well. Each day Ma washed, dried, starched and ironed sheets, pillowcases, shorts and shirts. She charged 12½ cents for each shirt, and less for the bed linens.

As the seventh child in the Bruneau family, Betsy had a front row seat to observe the comings and goings of her older siblings and she learned from their experiences and mistakes. She learned two things very early: having your own money could keep Pa from controlling your life, and not getting pregnant would keep some other man from controlling your life. Her thoughts and desires were unorthodox in the 1930s. After all, women were expected to marry as soon as possible, have children and serve their husbands. By the time Betsy was ten years old, three of her older sisters were married with children—and they had all been pregnant before they were married. Betsy knew she didn't want this kind of life for herself; she wanted something different. But she didn't know what it was yet.

Betsy had watched as her older siblings would beg Pa for things that he would never allow, and she understood quickly that having her own money might secure her freedom from his influence. But it was the Depression. The family never had much money and Betsy judged her father harshly for always giving ten percent of the family earnings to the Mormon Church. "We needed that money," she recalled, "but Pa never changed. He even took 10 percent of the money I earned and gave it to the Church." Betsy was unforgiving.

Betsy and her sister Margery made money delivering milk pails for Mrs. Jackshaw after school and on weekends. This neighbor had three cows, and Betsy delivered quart-sized pails of milk to five houses every day. She was paid five cents a day, thirty-five cents a week. This was the first money that she ever had as her own and she was determined to spend it on her first pair of new shoes from Myers Store on Main Street. "They were loafers," she remembered vividly, "with leather fringe on top." They cost $1.25, so Betsy brought them home after paying 25 cents down with a $1 to be paid over time. But Pa was outraged. He made her return the shoes because they were not completely paid for, and he made her give ten percent of her money to the Mormon Church.

"Never again," Betsy vowed. "Never again would Pa know how much money I have." And from that day on Betsy gave her money to her boyfriend, Bob Abrahamson, for safekeeping. Never again did she contribute to the Mormon Church. She continued to save the money she earned by delivering milk and babysitting for local families for 25 cents a night. Finally when she graduated from high school in 1938, Betsy used her own money to buy a high school ring, graduation announcement cards and a graduation dress. She was proud.

Two of Betsy's sisters had married into the Powell family, which ran a fishing resort on Saganaga Lake, northwest of Tower on the Minnesota-Canadian border.

Charlotte had married Frank Powell in 1929 and Dorothy Bruneau and Bill Powell were married in 1935. The resort was a busy place, and Pa Bruneau reasoned that Betsy and Margery should help their older sisters with the children and the chores during the summers. Betsy and Margery came for the first time in the summer of 1937. Betsy returned again in the summer of 1938 and stayed for good. Now there were three Bruneau sisters living on Saganaga Lake.

There were several reasons for Betsy to stay by then. There was no work in Tower because of the Depression and there was plenty of work at the resort. Betsy enjoyed the independent life she had working with Frank Powell and he welcomed her enthusiasm and hard work. Betsy had now identified something to do with her life that didn't involve getting pregnant or married. She lived in a small cabin at the resort; Frank, Charlotte and the children lived in the main lodge, and Bill, Dorothy and their two children lived in another cabin near the lodge.

She may not have known it at the time, but Frank Powell was destined to be a significant force in Betsy's life from that time forward.

Cabins and beach of Green Forest Resort in the 1930s

Chapter 2

Powell Family Beginnings ———————————

Frank Powell was an extraordinary man from an extraordinary family. His father, Jack, a Michigan native of Irish decent born in 1867, was abandoned by his father at a young age and sent by his mother to live with relatives who needed help on their farm in Wisconsin. In 1883 Jack left the farm at age 16 to work. Jack was young and strong, and like many men his age, he found work, first in northern logging camps and later for the railroad at the Winton-Ely Sawmill Rail in northern Minnesota. By his mid-20s, he knew the ways of farming, logging, cutting timber, running sawmills and fixing engines.

Around the turn of the century, Jack met Mary (Ak-Quay-Wa-ah-shek) Ottertail, a woman who was born at Crooked Lake, Ontario, in 1882 to Chief Ottertail and Caregaga of the Lac La Croix band of Ojibwe. Mary's people were native to this landscape, and Mary would be the helping hand that Jack needed to ensure that he could learn to live and stay in this country. She knew how to navigate the waterways, trap and hunt, prepare fur, make clothing, gather and store food and survive the various challenges of the seasons. She and Jack decided to spend their lives together when Mary was about 18—despite the disapproval of her Ojibwe family. Together, Jack and Mary moved north to live, work as trappers and start a family.

Jack Powell

Although the couple settled at the

eastern end of Saganagons Lake in Ontario, Canada, they were trappers, and trappers often traveled from camp to camp during trapping seasons in the spring and the fall. When they were not trapping they returned to their home, a 16' by 30' log cabin, where they raised five children. The third of those children was Frank Powell, born on December 5, 1906 as Benjamin Franklin Powell and named Mesh-kay-awsh, "The Wind that Comes Down to Earth," by Mary Ottertail. Jack never learned to speak Ojibwe and Mary never learned English. However, communication and learning were never compromised—they drew from their very different backgrounds to communicate and raise children skilled at living in the wilderness.

Mary Ottertail

Jack Powell and Mary Ottertail created a lifestyle that blended Mary's Ojibwe knowledge of living from the land with Jack's knowledge of the white man's world into a wealth of skills and opportunities that the Powell children would use for the rest of their lives. From their father, the Powell children learned to read and write, tend a garden, cut logs and build cabins, breed and manage sled dogs and operate and repair gasoline engines. Mary taught them how to gather berries and wild rice, snare rabbits, prepare furs, make clothing, make fishing nets and smoke meats. Together, Jack and Mary taught their children to hunt and fish and to

Jack Powell and his granddaughter, Minerva. She was the daughter of Tempest, Jack and Mary's youngest.

travel safely and reliably in the wilderness. Family life was focused on survival and Frank and the other children learned early to apply their skills to the business of living. Frank's childhood was a continuous, season-to-season ritual of living. It wasn't work—work was something you did for someone else—this was simply living. The Powell children, born into a life they loved, would use the knowledge their parents imparted all of their lives. Jack Powell was one of the first rangers in Quetico Provincial Park and his sons accompanied him on his long journeys through the wilderness. The Powells were known throughout the area as trusted woodsmen.

When the landscape was frozen, the family traveled the trap lines for food and fur and went to town for supplies. Frank and his brothers learned to travel cross-country to Kashabowie, 50 miles north of Saganagons, to sell furs and trade for supplies. Frank and Mike Powell, the two oldest boys, were often sent for supplies, as they were experienced and trusted wilderness travelers at a very young age. They would routinely travel to Harju's General Store on the Canadian National Railroad at Kashabowie, requiring at least two nights out on the trail alone.

In the spring and summer, when the landscape was transformed into a waterscape, the family traveled by canoe for fish, rice, berries and meat. Frank learned to hunt, smoke meat, make gill nets for fishing, gather and dry wild rice and berries, build canoes, repair small outboard motors and carve paddles. Before winter the family would cut firewood, re-stock the root cellar with the harvest from the garden, repair trapping shacks and knit hats and mittens.

Frank and his brother Mike, only a year apart in age, were inseparable as children and were never far from their father. When the Powell boys did leave the home of their childhood and start families of their own, they didn't move far.

Nearly all of the Powell children ended up settling around Saganaga Lake, at a time when the area was beginning to attract visitors interested in sport fishing. The Gunflint Trail had just opened, meandering inland from Grand Marais, Minnesota, to the Canadian border, bringing a group of primarily wealthy men to the region. The skills that the Powell children learned from their parents met the needs of these new visitors perfectly. Their wilderness skills also helped the Powell children make the transition from trapping to guiding, allowing them to stay in the area, make a living, and weather the changes that the years would bring to Saganaga Lake.

As Frank grew into a man, he mastered the skills that both of his parents provided. He could live comfortably in the wilderness, interact confidently in the outside world and turn his dreams and curiosities into opportunities. However,

Walter Plummer

Frank was close to three men in his life: his brother, Mike Powell, his son, Frankie, and Walter Plummer, his best friend. The Plummers were another Native American family that lived on Gunflint Lake. Walter was the son of Netowance, a Cree woman, and George Plummer, Sr. Walter had three siblings: George Jr., Lillian (Butchie) and Gladys. The family owned and operated a store and hotel next to the narrows on Gunflint Lake at the opening of Magnetic Bay. In the early days, Frank's family would travel down the Magnetic River to Gunflint Lake for supplies and mail. This is where the boys met.

Frank and Walter were inseparable. They hunted and trapped together every fall, walking or flying up to Walter's cabin at Mowe Lake. Every time Walter needed work or Frank needed help, they were together. Walter frequently stopped by to visit Betsy and Frank and stayed for days.

On September 19, 1949 Walter was found burned to death in his cabin on Gunflint Lake. It was a tragic day for Frank and Betsy as they had lost their best friend. Although the death was suspicious, it was never formally investigated.

Frank's best friend, Walter Plummer

Frank's true passion was flying. In the early 1920s, Jack Powell took his young family to Superior, Wisconsin to watch a World War I pilot demonstrate flying. Frank was awestruck. He thought of little else after that. He wanted to fly, he wanted to own an airplane and he wanted to see the land that he had grown to love—like a raven—from the sky.

By 1927, when he was 21, Frank had discovered a way to make his dreams come true. He began traveling back and forth to Tower, Minnesota to learn to fly planes with Oscar Ringnell and repair airplane engines with Dusty Rhodes at the airport on Lake Vermillion. This work was easy for Frank and he was flying almost immediately. As soon as he could, he bought his first plane. It was a Standard J1 (a World War I Jenny) airplane with skis and pontoons that he operated winter and summer.

Frank Powell

All his life Frank Powell attracted attention. He was a strong and competent man over six feet tall with dark hair and dark eyes. He was handsome, fun-loving, hard-working and adventurous. He was the perfect mix of Indian and Irish, a gentle, serious man with a hearty laugh who never lost his temper or argued with anyone. It was hardly surprising that the Bruneau girls from Tower noticed Frank and his brothers.

A Cow on the Water

Raising chickens and goats was simple enough, but transporting livestock across portages and in canoes was always a memorable experience. The Powell family adventures, which included transporting cows in canoes from Winton to Saganagons, were legendary. Unfortunately, the cows never lasted long—good grass was hard to find and the bulls were too temperamental and destructive.

From *A Life in Two Worlds*

"When Grandpa decided he needed a cow and a bull for the farm, the closest place to purchase them was at Winton, near Ely. He and my uncles, Mike and Frank, constructed a sturdy raft, which had been fastened across the top of the canoe; one regular canoe and one square stern canoe with a small outboard motor. He moved slowly and precariously down the lake to the first portage.

The cow was unloaded and tied to a tree. Grandpa and the boys

Mike Powell transporting the cow in a canoe

then went back and got the bull. They unloaded the bull at the portage and put a collar on him to which were attached two ropes. These ropes were fastened to the raft, which was detached from the canoes. With the cow following, the bull pulled the raft across the portage while Mike and Frank portaged the canoes. This tedious procedure was repeated on each of the ten portages it took to safely reach the farm." (Betty Powell Skoog and Justine Kerfoot, A Life in Two Worlds. Lake Nebagamon, Wisconsin: Paper Moon Publishing, 1996)

Tempest Powell milking the malnourished cow

From *Quetico Provincial Park: An Illustrated History*

"About July 1927, I was headed through Ottertrack Lake with Walter Anthony. I said, "What the hell is that comin' down the lake? Let's go look." It was Jack Powell and his sons Frank and Mike. They had a cow on the scow! The scow was about eight feet long; they had a canoe and a motor on each side of it. They had a halter on her, and her hind end was tied to both corners, so she wouldn't tip the whole works over. They were comin' up the lake! I said, "Where the hell you goin' with this?" (I knew Jack real well.)

"Well, you know we been eatin' dried milk for years, but we never get no fresh milk." I'd seen em that year cuttin' all the wild hay they could find. There was two or three big haystacks by their place on the east end of Saganagons. They had four hundred-pound sacks of oats, too, in the scow with the cow.

When they'd get to a portage, they'd put a horse collar with a couple of tumplines over the cow. They'd hook it up to the scow, and the cow would drag the scow over while they portaged the canoes and motors. So, I said, "Hell, we're gonna turn around—we gotta see that!" They were gonna go through Jasper and come out in Saganagons.

So, we went back with them to that portage. They hooked the cow up, and she hauled the boat up over the hill and down. We helped carry some of the packsacks across.

They got the cow home all right. I saw it about two weeks later. They had a barn already built for it. They were feedin' it wild hay and oats, but they finally had to shoot the cow that winter. She couldn't survive on that wild hay—got too skinny. So, old Jack shot the cow and they ate it." (Shirley Peruniak, Quetico Provincial Park: An Illustrated History. Atikokan, Ontario, Canada: Friends of Quetico Park, 2001)

Chapter 3

Green Forest Resort

Two Powell boys came to Tower in 1927—Frank came for flying lessons and his younger brother, Bill, came along to socialize. Frank and Bill stayed at Sody's Cabins on Lake Vermillion next to the Tower airport, and because there was no other place to eat, they ate all their meals at Frank Franson's Café in downtown Tower. The Bruneau sisters, Ginny, Alice and Charlotte, worked at Franson's where they met the Powell men. It didn't take long for Charlotte Bruneau to fall in love with Frank Powell. Within the year, as soon as she graduated from high school, Charlotte left with Frank to live in a cabin he had built on Beaver Lake near his parents. They were married in 1929. It must have been a difficult transition for Charlotte, who had no experience in the wilderness—the constant work, the travel from camp to camp, the unrelenting cold in winter and the heat and black flies in summer. They struggled. The market for fur was in decline and Frank could see that his brother, Mike, was making a better living as a fishing guide on Saganaga Lake than he was in the trapping business.

Because of Mike's success guiding fishermen, Frank thought that he, too, might become a guide to earn his living. Frank also wanted to open his own fishing resort to bring in some extra income. In 1932 there was no open sale of land in Canada, so Frank leased four acres of land on the north shore of Saganaga Lake from the Canadian Ministry of Natural Resources—two acres on the lake and two acres up the hill for ten dollars per acre per year. It was on this land that Frank started his own fishing resort and named it Green Forest Resort. He built three log cabins and soon was guiding fishing trips into the remote lake country, while Charlotte cooked and cleaned for their guests. Bill Powell and Dorothy Bruneau also moved in after they were married in 1935 to help run the resort.

Frank & Charlotte's Children

On April 13, 1931 Charlotte and Frank had their first child, Florence. Ruth followed five years later on February 8, 1936. Their third child, Francis, was born August 9, 1940 and Frank Jr. was born on December 28, 1943.

Although relationships were complicated at Green Forest Resort, Frank and Charlotte's children did get along with Betsy—Frank Jr. spent many hours working alongside Betsy. Nonetheless she was not particularly close with them.

Frank and Charlotte's girls: Ruth, Francis and Florence

The most tragic day in Frank Powell's life was September 9, 1958, when his son, Frankie (Frank Jr.), drowned by falling from his boat off of Windy Point on Saganaga Lake. After tirelessly dragging the lake looking for the body, Betsy and Frank recovered Frankie's body on the third day. They pulled young Frankie into the boat, covered him with a blanket and brought him back home; he was fourteen years old. The next day the Mounted Police arrived to transport young Frank's body to Thunder Bay for an autopsy. Frank Powell was never the same again.

Frank and Frankie

The place that Frank picked to live and work was perfect. It was both practical and inspirational. The resort sat deep inside a protective bay with a view of a rock-faced cliff to the east known as Raven's Rock, an island of white pine and a yellow sand beach facing south that caught shadows from the sun and the moon. The low areas were perfect for pulling boats onto the beach, logs from the water for the sawmill and ice cakes for storage in the icehouse. The deep-water drop-off was a perfect place to dock a boat. The property also lay along the portage to Frank's parents' home.

The beach at Green Forest Resort

Betsy worked in exchange for food and lodging but by the second summer she was also guiding fishermen with Bill and Frank. She knew very little about fishing but she could get guests down the lake, paddle them around to fish all day, land and filet the fish, prepare a shore lunch and get them home. Betsy was an eager and willing worker and Frank was her mentor. Soon she had learned to cut ice, set trap lines, build log cabins and run the sawmill. She made five dollars a day that she could keep for herself. She saved her money and started to dream about building her own cabin some day.

Having grown up in a household where his mother and sisters were equal partners with the men, it seemed natural to Frank that Betsy wanted to help with the work. Charlotte enjoyed Frank's success as a resort owner but was overwhelmed by the constant work and difficult conditions. Betsy, however, reveled in the work and as she and Frank traveled together for supplies and spent weeks in the bush on trap lines, her admiration turned to something deeper. Her

The blending of two families: the Bruneau sisters and the Powell men.
Back row: Mike Powell, Charlotte Bruneau Powell, Betsy Bruneau, Dorothy Bruneau Powell.
Front row: Frank Powell (head down), Ruth Powell, Marion Powell (Bill and
Dorothy's daughter), Florence Powell, and Bill Powell.

growing attraction to Frank overruled everything else. When Betsy and Frank became lovers, it strained her relationship with most members of her family and much of the lakeshore community. The costs in estrangement were high, but all her life she believed it had been worth it, that life with Frank Powell was the only life for her.

Frank was not as cut off from those he knew and loved. For many years he continued to live with Charlotte and the children. This was hard on everyone, but Betsy stayed because she could support herself by working at the resort, she felt she was part of a community and, quite simply, there was nowhere else to go.

The resort was popular with fisherman and continued to be successful. Life was very, very good at the resort in the late 1930s, but it didn't last. By the early 1940s, the effects of World War II were reaching the shores of Saganaga Lake. Gasoline was scarce and tourists had stopped coming north. The Powell men were too old to be drafted into the War, but they could no longer live from the land and raise their families without an income from guiding fishermen, so they had to move away to survive. Bill and Dorothy moved to Grand Marais in Minnesota to find work, and in the fall of 1940, Betsy and Frank moved to South St. Paul to work. Dr. Merle Thoreson, an owner at Shady Rest Cabin across from their resort at Saganaga, got them a job at the huge stockyards for Swift and Company. Betsy and Frank left the lake, while Charlotte and the children stayed behind. It was a matter of survival. In 1942 they too moved to St. Paul.

Frank worked killing hogs and smoking hams while Betsy washed and measured hog casings for sausage. They worked 11 hours every day, then had a Sunday off every other week. The money they made was either carefully saved in war bonds or used to support the family during those very hard times. It was a struggle for everyone.

St. Paul and its stockyards were a stark contrast to Saganaga Lake

Finally, the end of the war came. Rationing was lifted on many items and America's returning veterans were eager to resume living. In the spring of 1945 it was time to go home to Saganaga Lake and start over. But it would be different now: like fault lines shifting deep inside the earth, World War II changed the personal and professional landscape of Saganaga Lake. Bill and Dorothy moved to Scandia Bay and established their own fishing resort. Betsy and Frank had been saving and planning to expand Green Forest Resort and earn additional money by building cabins for people beginning to settle around the lake. And Frank and Charlotte now had four children to raise. Sorting out complicated relationships was not important then, establishing productive lifestyles was. Mostly there was a lot of work to do and Betsy and Frank were eager to get back to work on the land.

Betsy cashed in her war bonds to buy a new sawmill—a 1946 Bell saw from Kansas City, powered by the motor of a 1931 Model A Ford that Frank rigged. The new saw was shipped to Duluth from Kansas City unassembled. Brazell Freight picked it up and delivered it to the end of the Gunflint Trail. From there, Betsy and Frank hauled it on their sled across the lake to the resort in the winter of 1946. To power the sawmill, Frank took off the back wheels of the Model A and ran a shaft straight into the universal joint. A 24" pulley with a 6" face and a 50' endless belt drove the saw blade. The saw blade was a 42" inserted-tooth blade.

There were already contracts to build four log cabins and a sawmill was essential for finishing the cabins. The sawmill would also provide the opportunity to build frame cabins—a type of construction that used less timber and could be adapted to any site. Betsy started to dream again about building her own cabin, but first she needed to make money.

Frank indulged his passion for flying when he bought a new airplane—a de Havilland Gypsy Moth with two cockpits. The airplane landed on skis in the winter and pontoons in the summer. He used the plane to transport fishermen to

The islands of Sag that Frank and Betsy missed while in St. Paul

Betsy and Frank in front of one of Frank's Aeronca Champion

remote areas and to fly to Kashabowie, Ontario, for supplies. Frank was a happy man. He was home again, he was flying again and would give airplane rides to anyone who wanted to go.

Charlotte resumed her chores cleaning cabins and cooking for guests at Shady Rest, Chippewa Inn and Louie Finn's, all the while raising the children. Charlotte, Frank and the four children continued to live in the old lodge building. Betsy continued to live in one of the cabins. Relationships remained complicated: Frank loved Betsy, but he also loved his children. Frank wanted his children to learn about living the way he had learned from his mother and father.

Betsy continued to be the outcast of most of the Powell family, although she and her sister Dorothy remained close friends throughout their lives. Betsy's days and evenings were filled with work. She loved Frank, she loved the work and she loved the fact that she could support herself. It was enough.

Frank & Flying

Frank and one of his flying machines

Frank pursued his love of flying for 28 years in a series of airplanes, from his first Jenny he bought in 1927 to the de Havilland Gypsy Moth purchased in 1946, followed by a 64-horsepower (hp) and finally an 85-hp Aeronca Champion. But he stopped flying forever in 1955 after Betsy gave him an ultimatum: "Either stop flying or stop drinking," she demanded. It was a tough decision. Frank loved flying more than anything else he knew how to do, but he didn't love it more than drinking.

Frank landing the Standard J1 (WWI Jenny) airplane on Saganagons Lake

Chapter 4

Seasons of Living and Working

By 1946 Betsy and Frank had been away from Saganaga for five years and they missed being home. They were now determined to do whatever it would take to stay there forever. Betsy Bruneau and Frank Powell were even more established as partners now: they made plans together, they worked together and they cared for each other. This was a relationship of hard work and mutual respect, just like that of Jack Powell and Mary Ottertail. There was little that they could not accomplish together.

The fishing business took first priority after the war, but building cabins for new land owners on Saganaga and Northern Light Lakes would fill in all the spare hours of every day. They were busy and content, winter and summer.

Frank was the boss. He was a serious worker who would begin each day with an announcement of "what needed to be done." He didn't write it down, he didn't explain it in great detail, he just started working and he expected Betsy to follow him and figure it out. Frank would plan projects in his head for

Betsy's cabin at Green Forest Resort

days and then just start. This was the way he constructed airboats, barges, airplane hangers and cabins. It was frustrating to Betsy who always wanted to talk about what they were going to do and how they were going to do it. Frank couldn't explain anything but he could do everything. Betsy would buy books on building cabins and mixing cement from Montgomery Wards and study them; Frank would figure it out by trial and error. His daily decision-making about what to do was dictated by the seasons of the year, the weather and the hundreds of interrelated tasks required to guide fishermen, build cabins and maintain a resort business all at the same time.

Betsy hauling gas, a never-ending chore

On Saganaga Lake there were three seasons of work: winter (ice), summer (water) and the "seasons in-between." These interim seasons were in some ways the most difficult, since travel was often impossible until the ice had completely melted or the lake was completely frozen.

Winter on Saganaga started with the ice that usually formed between November 20 and December 10. In 1962 the lake didn't freeze until December 12th, and in 1951 it froze on November 18.

Winter provided a season of harvest. In early winter Frank would hunt for deer, bear and moose and trap for beaver, mink and muskrat. Betsy would contribute by setting rabbit snares in the woods and fish hooks through the ice. With this harvest they smoked or canned the meat for food and they dried and stretched the furs for market. Then they settled into the other chores of winter—cutting ice, sawing and hauling timber, and engine repair. Ice was harvested from the lake in late December or early January every year from 1950 to about 1965. Timber was harvested in winter and logs for the log cabins were moved from the woods to the shoreline or from the shoreline to the sawmill. Engines were repaired in winter and, as the years progressed, there were more and more engines to fix.

Motors powered an assortment of winter travel vehicles known as airboats, snow fleas, motor toboggans, ski sleds and Sno Travelers (the first snowmobile). Traveling across snow and lake ice in a motor-ized vehicle was a dream for anyone living on a landscape as remote as Saganaga Lake in the winter. Frank tried to make every vehicle he owned move across the snow; he invented and designed a few and repaired or remodeled them all. Vehicles de-signed for winter travel, however, inevitably pushed the limits of technology, which meant that they were always breaking down.

Betsy, Frank, and Frankie weathering the cold indoors on a -40° day

Winter was hard on these early machines, and there were even a few days when the weather forced both Betsy and Frank inside—when the temperature was 30 to 40 degrees below zero and the wind was blowing. Betsy would stay indoors to knit hats and mittens, crochet pot holders, sew shirts and pants, bake bread, wash clothes, write to guests and read. For a few years Betsy even tried paint-ing—paint-by-number. Betsy and Frank would play cards and cribbage, sleep and listen to the radio. Sometimes Frank would play along with his fiddle.

Winter ended when the ice went out, and ice-out on Saganaga Lake usually happened between May 1 and May 10. But, in 1950 and 1966 the ice didn't disappear until May 22. The earliest ice-out was in 1955 and 1958 when it melted on April 21. When the ice was gone, fishermen and lake residents arrived almost immediately; they all lived in warmer climates and were anxious to get "on the water." Especially during these interim seasons, Betsy and Frank's activities were very much dictated by the weather conditions and the timing of the ice outs which in turn determined when the fishermen arrived.

The first chores of spring included changing the airplane's skis and replacing

Winter Travel Inventions

Propeller-driven air sleds

A popular approach to winter travel was to take an airplane fuselage, mount it on three skis, attach a propeller to the back of it and ride. These vehicles were used for many years by residents and visitors. The first snow machine at Green Forest Resort was a 1958 Polaris Sno Traveler with a Clinton 10-hp motor. Frank quickly replaced this motor with a Kohler 10-hp

1958 Polaris Sno Traveler

motor. The snow machines were used to haul logs, lumber, 55-gallon barrels of gasoline, supplies and children.

Frank built an airboat he called the Snow Flea, inspired by the Florida swamp buggies he'd heard about. With its 65-hp Continental aircraft engine and tempered aluminum sheet frame, the Snow Flea could slide over snow and ice and cruise across water while dodging ice floes. Betsy would drag her foot along the ice as a brake. This vehicle underwent several modifications over the years, including turning the propeller around so it wasn't spinning right behind the driver's head. Betsy and Frank used this craft until 1975 to get the mail and make winter trips to Northern Light Lake.

Frank in the Snow Flea

them with pontoons, preparing the garden, repairing or building boats and cleaning cabins at the resort and for other lake residents. If Betsy and Frank were lucky, there were a couple of weeks between the melting of the ice and the fishing opener to give them time for hauling. They hauled logs to cabin sites; building supplies from the boat landing; and gasoline, propane and cabin residents back-and-forth across the lakes.

Too often, however, the ice would go out on or after the fishing opener and the hauling chores were intermingled with the duties of guiding fishermen. In addition to clean cabins, the fishermen required ice or propane for refrigeration, minnows for bait, gas for their boats, prepared meals and shore lunches, and a great deal of conversation. There would always be at least two parties at the resort at any given time during the spring and summer—May and June were frantic.

Summer was the season for cabin building. Betsy and Frank sawed lumber; cut, hauled and peeled logs; installed windows, doors and screens; shingled roofs; built furniture and beds; and built docks, wood sheds, outhouses. They also oiled or painted the walls and ceilings of the cabins to prevent cracks and to preserve the wood. Cabin building chores were as numerous as the fishermen.

Frank's plane loaded with supplies and fishermen headed to Saganagons

By late fall, as the season of ice approached and the fishermen left, Betsy and Frank would change the airplane floats to skis, close down cabins, do some hunting for ducks and moose and then leave the lake for a vacation. The only time they left Saganaga was in the fall, when transportation across the lake was difficult for fishermen and guests. Betsy and Frank would take this opportunity to travel to Grand Marais and Fort William where they would stay with friends, see a movie and have dinner. Betsy would also travel back to Tower, Minnesota to see her family and get a permanent from a hairdresser there. When the ice returned to begin another winter, Betsy and Frank came home to start a new year.

Despite the hard work and long days, Betsy was inspired every day of her life by the beauty around her at Saganaga. Her inspiration found an outlet in 1945 when she was given her first camera by Bud Potter, a guest at the resort. It was a 35mm Minolta Pocket Autopak 460TX. She started by taking pictures of clouds, her favorite subject, and she took pictures nearly every day. These images span more than 60 years, punctuating her stories and providing evidence for a life unimagined on this landscape today.

Frank traveling on Saganaga Lake

Don Brazell

Don Brazell became a staple in the lives of those living in the wilderness of Saganaga. From delivering mail, resort guests, or even Betsy's new sawmill, Don and his services have become a legend in the area.

From *Woman of the Boundary Waters*

"In April 1933 Don had started making weekly trips from Grand Marais to all the resorts on the Trail as a beer service. The resort operators sighed with relief. No longer must they travel the narrow, hilly, twisty road for every needed item....Over the years Don became a vital link who made it possible for the resorts to operate successfully. In between runs he graciously shopped for us and picked up innumerable small items from personal packages to a spool of thread or a package of bandages. His arrival was like the stagecoach coming. All the neighbors came from across the lake to socialize or to pick up an item Don might have for them. Don became authorized to carry the mail officially on a Star Route, after the necessary surveys were made and forms filled out. Our mail service ballooned to twice a week in summer and once a week in winter. (Justine Kerfoot, Woman of the Boundary Waters [1986; reprinted Minneapolis: University of Minnesota Press, 1994])

Brazell's delivery truck

Chapter 5

The Trapper's Life

Trapping is what brought white men to this country in the beginning. European fashion had depleted the supply of beaver from Europe and the North American continent offered an unending supply of furs throughout a vast system of waterways from Lake Superior to Lake Athabasca. Frank grew up trapping as a child, and continued to trap into his adulthood until—and even after—the fishing resort was opened. When Frank Powell was a boy, trapping could support a family. However, it took several hundred square miles of trapping country, and life as a family was spent traveling from trapping shack to trapping shack by dogsled throughout the winter months. Fur was the only source of family income and they worked hard to make money.

Trapping was indeed hard work. Prior to WWII, Betsy and Frank spent the majority of their time in the fall, winter and spring trapping or maintaining trapping shacks and working in the traditional Powell trapping grounds north of Saganagons Lake and east of Quetico Park.

Frank and a trapped marten

A trapping shack

In this area Frank and his brothers maintained at least six trapping shacks, and the trade continued to support them into the 1930s.

Trapping shacks were rustic log structures, measuring about 10' by 12', depending on the height of the trees in the area. The roof was covered with birch bark and moss and walls were caulked with moss. Inside, cedar shakes covered a log floor, while a small table, split log bench and two log sleeping frames covered with boughs constituted the furniture. A steel stove provided both heat and a cooking surface and a kerosene lamp was the single source of light. Everything else that was needed was carried into the shacks during the trapping season. It was considered foolish to trust that someone else would leave behind what was needed, or that if something was left in a trapping shack on an earlier trip that it

Walter Plummer's trapping shack

Frank skinning a bear

would still be there.

Each trip to a trap line lasted two to three weeks. Betsy and Frank each carried heavy #4 Duluth packs filled with food, traps, clothing and the snowshoe hare blankets made by Frank's mother that they used as sleeping bags. They traveled on 12" x 30" Tubbs snowshoes carrying these packs for 20 miles or more between shacks. They wore woolen union-suits and leather choppers and boots from L.L. Bean—but there was nothing to protect them from the wind. Weather was always a factor; if they were unable to reach the next shack by nightfall, they camped out in the woods inside a tent Betsy had made from aircraft linen. With a fire built just outside the tent flap, they slept comfortably in their rabbit fur sleeping bags placed over pine boughs.

The trapping shacks provided a warm place to prepare the hides, which was Frank's job, since Betsy could never get the hang of scraping the hide without cutting through it. After several weeks, they'd pack up everything and snowshoe out, usually to Jack Powell's place, where they'd leave their hides and return to Saganaga to regroup before the next trip.

In Frank's early adulthood, the market for beaver was recovering from the impacts of World War I. The beaver populations were high and trapping remained a reliable way to support a family. By the end of the 1920s, trapping

Frank holding a bobcat before it is skinned

became a highly profitable occupation as the price of furs rose. A beaver pelt that sold for $21 in 1921 was going for $60-80 by 1927.

However, Frank's success at trapping and its ability to sustain a family soon dwindled. In the late 1930s the Depression nearly eliminated the market for furs. The trade that had sustained Frank throughout his childhood and early adulthood was no longer capable of bringing in a good income. Fortunately, as the trapping business declined, the fishing business emerged. The Powells were woodsmen of renowned fame in this country and their services as fishing guides soon provided an attractive alternative to trapping.

Despite their success as fishing guides and resort owners, Betsy and Frank did not stop trapping for added income until the 1950s, although they continued to occasionally trap for their own use. With the fur market on the decline and government regulation on the increase, they got out of trapping altogether.

Trapping Shack Locations

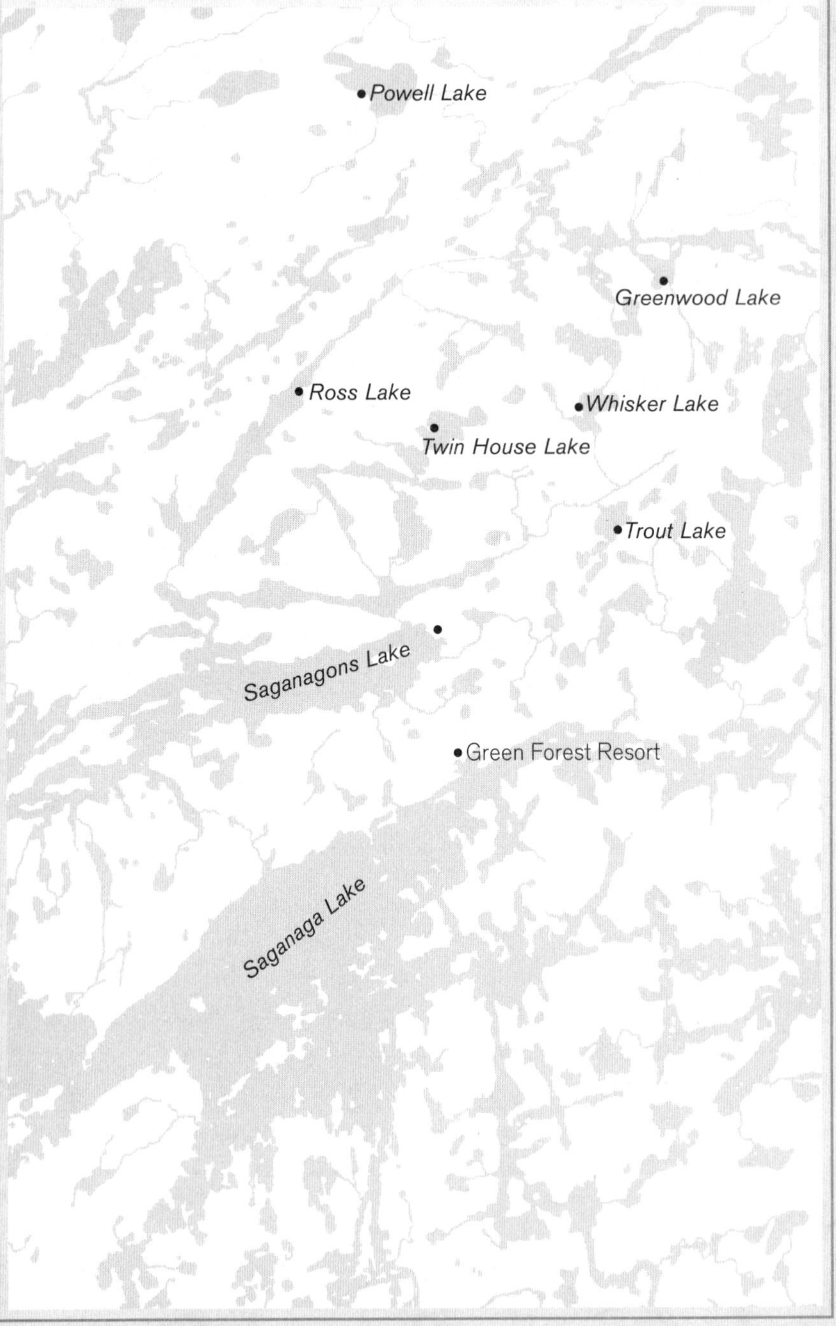

• Powell Lake

• Greenwood Lake

• Ross Lake

• Whisker Lake

• Twin House Lake

• Trout Lake

Saganagons Lake •

• Green Forest Resort

Saganaga Lake

Betsy's Instructions for Trapping a Beaver

In order to trap a beaver, first scout for beaver activity in the late fall before freeze-up. Look for lodge buildings and dams and identify the beaver runaway channels from the beaver houses. When you have picked a site, bait a #14 trap with a fresh poplar branch about one inch in diameter. Place the trap carefully to ensure that when the beaver is caught, he will be pulled under the water by the weight of the trap.

When you return to the trap, you should find that the beaver has died by drowning and will be completely submerged under the water, away from predators and away from the effects of freezing. Return to the trapping shack with the beaver and skin him.

Cut off his feet and tail. Slit his hide from his chin down, cut off the head and skin the hide from the body. With an ordinary skinning knife, scrape the flesh from the hide and stretch the hide on a wooden hoop made from ash or swamp maple. Lace the hide to the hoop with twine in a beaver needle about five inches long. Dry the stretched fur in the trapping shack. When it is dry, roll it up for transport home.

Beaver meat is very good. The tail is roasted immediately, sliced and eaten. Larger sections of the carcass, like the legs, tenderloins and sirloins, are cut and packed out.

Chapter 6

The Fishermen & Fishing Guides of Saganaga ———

Learning to fish in Jack Powell's family was like learning to cut and split wood or learning to trap—it was a chore of daily life, a harvest from the land that supplied the family with food. The Powell family didn't fish with poles, they fished with nets in the style of the Ojibwe. The Powell children grew up knowing which fish lived where in all seasons of the year; it was a knowledge that would prove essential for their transition into the next lifestyle on this landscape.

Because of their upbringing, the Powell children were well prepared to guide the kind of people coming into the region. Prior to the war years these were doctors, lawyers and clergymen, as they were the only ones who could afford the time or the expense of traveling this far into the woods to fish. After WW II, most anyone could afford the trip north. But all these visitors had limited time, little knowledge of the country and few wilderness skills. These men were not fishing for food, they were fishing for adventure. For them, catching a large fish on a wilderness lake, spending the night under the stars, cooking fish over a campfire and hearing the loons sing in the moonlight was an experience worth paying for. Frank and Mike Powell started guiding as soon as recreational fishermen arrived on these waters, and they arrived in increasing numbers as the Gunflint Trail was completed from Grand Marais, Minnesota to Saganaga Lake in the early 1930s.

The lake's lodges promised that their guests would catch fish they could brag about for years. The limit for fish was five fish per-person-per-day-per-species-of-fish, and guests usually caught their limit. In order to achieve this goal, fishing guides were paid to spend time with a group of men canoeing in the area or fishing the lakes. Frank and Bill transported guests to the lodge

In the early 1950s, a day's worth of fishing at Green Forest Resort would cost $18.50: $12.00 for the guiding, $4.00 for two canoes and $2.50 for the use of the motor. Here, the Lambert party is pictured just before they set out for a day filled with fishing.

and guided them all day on Saganaga, Saganagons and Northern Light lakes in search of trout and northern pike. In spite of the Depression, the fishing business provided an income for the wilderness and fishing guides of Saganaga.

With the success of the fishing industry in the mid-1930s, Frank and Bill and their wives were busy with Green Forest Resort on the Canadian shore of Saganaga Lake. Their resort offered tourists the opportunity to fish in Canadian waters and to stay farther out on the lake. Outboard motors in the 1930s were not particularly useful for fishing as they were unable to idle long without over-heating because their water pumps didn't work well at slow speeds. So most days of fishing required that Frank, Bill or Betsy row the guests around the fishing grounds all day.

The fishing business waned due to scarcity of gasoline in the 1930s. Gasoline was a critical supply: guests needed gasoline to travel to Grand Marais and up the Gunflint Trail, and Betsy and Frank needed it for their outboard motors. When gas was available it had to be hauled a great distance across the water .

A winter's catch

and across the portage to Saganagons on Frank or Betsy's back. Thus, its use was limited to running guests down the lakes and back. World War II eventually slowed the sport fishing industry to a halt. There was no longer any way to make money on this landscape and few were able to live there anymore without some income or without motorized transportation. Much of Saganaga's community of trappers, guides and Indians left the area during the war and did not return.

Despite the lull in the fishing industry during WWII, business quickly picked up in the mid-1940s and 1950s. People were making money again, and the average citizen could afford to venture north. Also important, gasoline rationing was lifted and new outboard motors made boat travel more reliable. Fishermen drove up the Gunflint Trail and some of them flew into the area. In fact, the small town of Ely, Minnesota, a jumping-off point for the wilderness, had the largest float-plane base in the country in 1949. The war had trained thousands of pilots who could use their skills to fly people into the wilderness to hunt and fish.

After the war, Betsy and Frank expanded the resort to accommodate more fishermen. From 1950 to 1955 they tore down the old resort and built five new cabins on Saganaga and three new cabins on Saganagons where the old cabins used to sit. Frank loved to fly his guests in his plane over the country where he'd grown up, land on a wilderness lake to discover what lay beneath, then come home at the end of the day with smiling guests who'd caught their limit of fish. Staying at Green Forest Resort could be an event to remember for the rest of one's life.

Betsy and Frank holding up some walleyes after a successful day of fishing on Saganaga

A fishing party in one of the barges Frank made

Frank built the barges that he used on Saganagons Lake for fishing. These were flat-bottomed boats made of cedar, like some Frank had seen on That Man Lake in 1949 when there was a drilling crew stationed there looking for silver. He copied the boats from memory and built his own. He used three 16' cedar skiffs and one 18-footer. He also built a 24' cedar barge that was 3' deep and 5½' wide. These boats could haul several men and their fishing gear safely. Frank also built his own skiffs and canoes for use at the resort.

At the end of each day the fishermen would retire to their cabins and invite Frank over for a few drinks. The guests liked to stay up late into the night, pouring whiskey, playing cards and cribbage and listening to Frank tell stories about his life. Frank was the reason many of the guests would come back again and again; to his guests Frank represented a real man in the real wilderness. The whiskey they supplied kept the late-night stories coming, but it also kept Frank from fully contributing to running the resort with Betsy in the daylight hours.

It was the business partnership between Betsy and Frank that built and maintained the guiding business of Green Forest Resort after the war, but it was successful because of the personal relationship between Betsy and Frank. In their partnership, Frank was the woodsman and the storyteller while Betsy was the businesswoman and the worker. Without Betsy, Frank would have neglected to charge his guests enough money to run the resort. He would have given away what money he had or spent it on whiskey and the chores required to keep fishermen fishing day after day would have been neglected. Betsy and Frank needed one another. Fishermen came north initially because of the country and the fish awaiting them. However, they stayed and returned because of Betsy and Frank.

As the business grew, however, the fishing started changing for two reasons: walleyes and snowmobiles. The lake had been stocked with walleye in the 1930s and, by the 1950s, surpassed trout and smallmouth bass as the fish of choice. Betsy and Frank began to harvest ice in the winter, which allowed fishermen to take fresh fish home. The walleye brought more fishermen and soon, with the invention of the snow machine, the fishermen started to come in the winter as well as in the summer. In the mid-1950s, early versions of snow machines of varying reliability began appearing on the ice and by the 1960s winter fishing had become a permanent service of Green Forest Resort.

Life was good, business was booming and Betsy and Frank had successfully survived the transition from the self-sufficient, subsistence culture they had learned from the Ojibwe to the self-sufficient lifestyle of a business owner in the service industry. They had accomplished this without leaving their home or the landscapes and waterscapes of Saganaga Lake. The continuing pressure to adapt and change, however, was just beginning.

The largest fish Betsy caught were 18 to 20 lb. walleyes and 25 to 30 lb. trout

Fishing

Fishing was the main activity from May through October. Betsy described her daily routine:

1. Get up at 5 a.m. and pack the gear.

2. Walk the 2½-mile portage to Saganagons Lake, stopping along the way to harvest minnows and set traps for the next day's minnows.

3. Prepare the barges for the day: attach motors, load all gear, get fishermen settled and push off.

4. Motor to a fishing spot, wait for a fish to be hooked, land and filet the fish and keep fishing.

5. Prepare a shore lunch of beans, coffee and the fish caught that morning.

6. At the end of the day, return to the portage, unload the barges and put the motors away.

7. Haul the gear and the day's fish over the portage.

8. Clean and prepare the afternoon catch for dinner.

9. Clean up the gear and get ready for the next day.

10. At 5 a.m., start all over again.

The Fishing Grounds

Betsy and Frank fished all of the lakes north and east of Saganaga:

Big Lake	Little Long Lake
Sand Lake	Deer Lake
High Lake	South Fowl Lake
Elevation Lake	Ross Lake
Head Lake	That Man Lake
Koss Lake	Beaver Lake
Big Sandy Lake	Plummes Lake
Little Whitefish Lake	Whitefish Lake
Sandstone Lake	Mowe Lake
Northern Light Lake	Baril Lake
Greer Lake	Wye Lake
Squeers Lake	Kawnipi Lake
Mack Lake	Red Fox Lake
Titmarsh Lake	Gunflint Lake
Marabouf Lake	

The trout in Elevation Lake were of particular interest, as they were native fish (the lake had never been artificially planted). These trout looked like a mountain trout with a square tail.

The Gunflint Trail

The North Shore Road from Duluth to Grand Marais (now Highway 61) was not passable by vehicle until 1900, and the Gunflint Trail from Grand Marais to Gunflint Lake was not passable until 1927. In 1930, the Gunflint Trail was extended to SeaGull Lake and on to Saganaga Lake when Russell Blankenburg and Art Nunstead started building lodges on Saganaga Lake. Russell built End of the Trail Lodge and Art built Chic Wauk Lodge. Together they built and maintained the road to Saganaga as a toll road. The toll was $2.00 per car or $0.50 per person.

Beginning around 1930 sports fishermen were discovering Saganaga Lake. Saganaga was the "end of the road"—as far north as one could go in Minnesota and still be in the United States. The lodges on Saganaga Lake provided the ultimate wilderness experience, now accessible because of the Gunflint Trail.

With direct access to the Gunflint Trail from Saganaga Lake established, Chik Wauk Lodge became the "landing" for Saganaga Lake residents, and freight and mail were delivered here. By 1955, when Frank stopped flying, the Gunflint Trail was the only route to the outside world.

See overall map on pages 8 and 9.

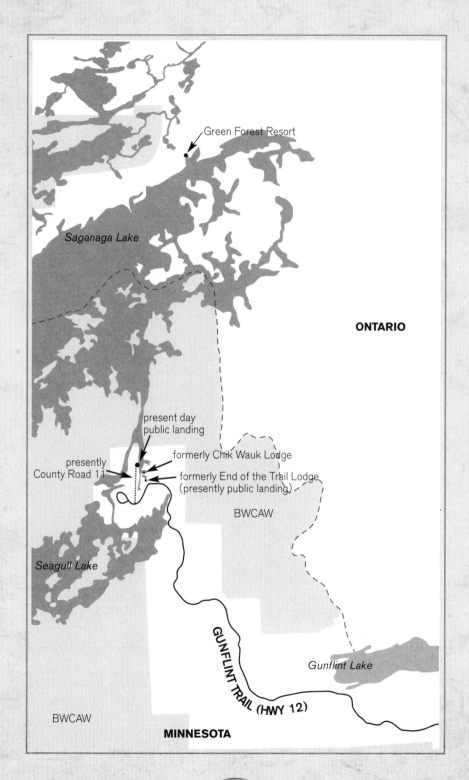

Green Forest Resort

Saganaga Lake

ONTARIO

present day
public landing

formerly Chik Wauk Lodge

presently
County Road 11

formerly End of the Trail Lodge
(presently public landing)

BWCAW

Seagull Lake

GUNFLINT TRAIL (HWY 12)

Gunflint Lake

BWCAW

MINNESOTA

Boundary Waters Canoe Area

The Wilderness Bill was passed in 1964 and from it the National Wilderness Preservation System—a system which included the BWCA—was created. Major changes around the lake began in 1965 when Saganaga Lake residents within the BWCA were forced to sell their homes and businesses to the government and leave the lake. The government tore down the buildings or burned them down in order to make the area a wilderness preserve. The definition of wilderness established by law in the United States was different than anything Frank and Betsy had ever known.

"A wilderness, in contrast with those areas where man and his own works dominate the landscape, is hereby recognized as an area where the earth and its community of life are untrammeled by man, where man himself is a visitor who does not remain..." [The Wilderness Act of 1964; Public Law 88-577, 78 Stat 890, 16 U.S.C. 1131-1136 Section 2 (c)].

The Boundary Waters Canoe Area Wilderness in northeastern Minnesota sits along the border between the United States and Canada. It holds some 1,100 lakes in its 1.1 million acres and people are allowed entry only as visitors. The Boundary Waters joins Canada's Quetico Provincial Park, a wilderness of almost equal size. Together they make up a 2-million-acre park whose residents include wolves, moose, bear, lynx, deer, beaver and loons.

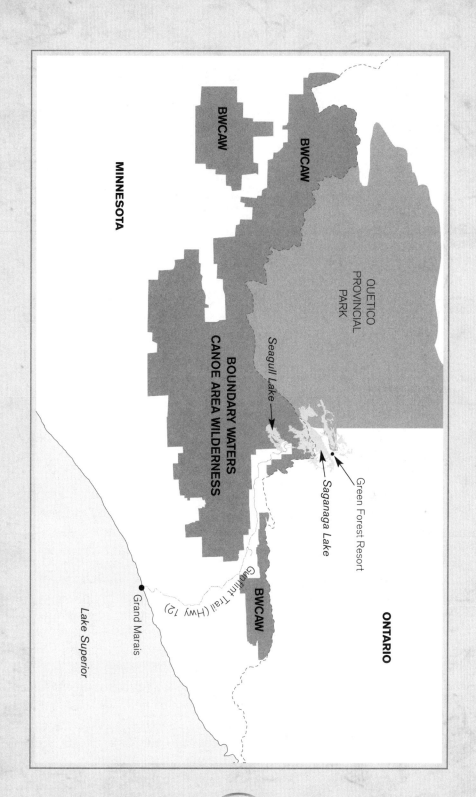

MINNESOTA

BWCAW

BWCAW

QUETICO
PROVINCIAL
PARK

ONTARIO

Seagull Lake

BOUNDARY WATERS
CANOE AREA WILDERNESS

Green Forest Resort

Saganaga Lake

BWCAW

Gunflint Trail (Hwy 12)

Grand Marais

Lake Superior

Chapter 7

Cabin Building

Open sale of land started on the north side of Saganaga, in Canada, in May, 1945. Betsy and Frank bought the four acres of land that they had been leasing from the government along with an additional five acres to allow for expansion of the resort. Most of the new people who were purchasing land around Saganaga and Northern Light lakes in the mid- to late-1940s weren't homesteaders, but instead preferred to take up residence only in the summer; these summer cabins were sanctuaries.

In this new life, Betsy and Frank were valued mostly because they accommodated other people's dreams by providing a convenient wilderness vacation and place in the woods that was maintained and cared for. Betsy and Frank built, finished and repaired cabins, guided fishermen, hauled supplies back and forth for cabin owners and their guests and opened or closed lake cabins for the season. Frank also indulged these new residents of Saganaga by regaling them for hours with the stories of his childhood in the wilderness.

In the beginning, log buildings were built in a manner that Frank had learned from his father. Betsy and Frank charged from $2,000 to $5,000 (depending on the size) for each log cabin they built. This covered the cost of logs and labor—at about 5 cents an hour.

Cabin building was a time-consuming and intricate process, requiring lots of patience and perseverance. In order to build a solid cabin, good craftsmanship was essential, although the season in which the work was done was also important. If done out of season, the logs could turn black and the whole cabin could be ruined. Betsy explains the delicate and detailed process of cabin building that she and Frank followed.

Obtaining a Permit in the U.S.
to Build on Saganaga

From *Sunset Cabin Plan Book*

"To obtain a cabin permit from the Forest Service, write or call on the Supervisor or nearest Ranger of the particular forest in which you think you'd like to live. Application for a permit may be made in writing to the Forest Supervisor, or Forest Ranger, specifying the location of the property, the use to be made of it (summer cabin, hotel, or resort) and the estimated cost of the improvement you intend to make.

Permits are granted strictly on a "first-come, first-served" basis. The cost—and this will amaze you—averages about $15 per year for cabin sites, depending on the size and location of the property. Each permit is renewable annually. You may sell your cabin at any time, but the transaction must be approved by the Forest Service.

When you apply for a permit, you must agree to install permanent improvements costing at least $500, including labor. All buildings and roofs must be painted, oiled or stained. If paint is used, the color must harmonize with the forest background and be approved by the Forest Supervisor. That does not mean that everything has to be brown and green, but the forest is no place for a pink stucco cottage.

Permanent construction must be completed by the end of the second season after the permit is issued. Cabins built under "special use" permits must be occupied at least 15 days each year by the permittee or his family, unless special arrangement is made with the Forest Service." [Ralph P. Dillon, *Sunset Cabin Plan Book* (San Francisco: Lane Publishing, 1946)]

Construction Before the Sawmill

The process of building a log cabin went something like this:

1. First scout a building site. Find a level site with plenty of healthy, overhanging trees to support winches and bedrock to support the logs. Select trees for cutting. These must be about 10" in diameter, straight without much tapering, standing close to the water and uphill. The incline is necessary because two people pulling a log that weighs more than 1,000 pounds by hand can only move it down to the water with the help of gravity. Saganaga has plenty of Norway Pines that fit this description, although Jack Pine and spruce are just as acceptable.

2. When 150 trees are marked with a blaze mark, call the Canadian Ministry of Natural Resources and wait for their representative to fly in, mark the selected trees with paint and give permission to cut them.

3. Cut the trees by hand with a cross-cut saw, remove the branches and move the logs to the shoreline in the fall or early winter. The best way to move a 1,000-pound log is to peel one side of the log for about one third of its diameter along its whole length, lay little sticks on the ground perpendicular to the log, roll the log onto the sticks with the peeled surface facing down and then pull it to shore with cant hooks. Notify the Ministry of Natural Resources again, so a scaler

Moving the logs with cant hooks in the water

can fly in and calculate the cost of the wood by tallying up the board feet in each log. They usually charge about one third of the current market value of the lumber or logs. The logs are then branded with an S.

4. Although the logs will be moved to the building site in the spring, pull the logs onto the surface of the ice and put them in a boom. Then, in the spring when the ice melts, the logs are ready to go. If this can't be done, roll the logs into the water in the spring for transport to the building site.

5. Once the logs are floating on open water, and have stopped rolling, set a 4" metal spike into each one. (If you set the spike before you float the log, it is as likely to roll upside-down as right-side up.) Once the logs are spiked, tie them together by their spikes and then slowly drag them through the water behind a boat with a 5 hp outboard motor to the building site. Early morning or late evening is best when the wind is down. About 75' from shore, release the boom and get out of the way as they drift toward land.

Pulling a boom of logs through the water

6. Pull the logs from the water with a motorized winch strung on a line that pivots on a pulley up in a tree and then down to the log in the water. One at a time stack the logs on the shoreline.

7. They're now ready for peeling, a job that is accomplished with a draw knife; then scribe them with an axe. Betsy explains that peeling is particularly important—you have to go deep into the wood and the logs have to be peeled in late fall or early winter or the wood turns black over time.

8. Lay the logs on the foundation and begin to build the walls of the cabin. including the gable ends, by securing them to one another with spikes. Place the spikes on either side of windows and doors and at the center of any long

spans of log. Bore a ³/₈" hole about 5" to 6" into the wood and then another ¼" hole through that log into the next log. With a pick hammer drive the spike deep into the hole. This is enough to keep the logs in place. After World War II steel spikes were used, but before the war Frank used wooden pegs.

Building the walls of a log cabin for Ed Kohl in 1948

The era of log cabin building, however, was coming to an end. Frame cabins took the place of log homes in the mid-1940s, when Betsy used her wartime earnings to purchase a sawmill. With the new sawmill and the availability of construction materials from the outside, many more cabins could be built easier, faster, with fewer trees and on building sites that were not suitable for log structures.

A finished log cabin, all built by hand

The end of log cabin building was brought on by the purchase of a sawmill after World War II. Here, logs are stacked at the sawmill ready to be turned into boards for building frame cabins.

Construction After the Sawmill

Frame cabin construction went like this:

1. Cut logs into 10' or 20' lengths and stack them at the shoreline in late fall or early winter until they can be transported to the sawmill.

2. In the spring, roll the logs into the lake, set an 8" to 10" metal spike into the ends of each one, tie them together and tow them across the water by boat.

3. At the sawmill near Green Forest Resort, pull the spikes from the logs, drag the logs from the water with a winch and stack them to dry.

Pulling logs out of the water using an 8 hp Clinton motor. Stacked logs drying for the sawmill (below).

4. From the logs cut boards into lengths and cut beams and framing lumber. Save the sawdust for insulation in the icehouses and leftover slabs of wood for firewood.

Frank and Betsy running the 8-hp Briggs & Stratton engine to cut beams and planks at their sawmill. Betsy then stacks the lumber to be used for frame cabins.

5. Push the cut planks through a 12" Bell saw planer powered by an 8-hp Briggs & Stratton engine, then stack the lumber and let it dry for at least a summer.

6. Move the lumber to the building sites by stacking the lumber into an 18' Peterborough square-stern canoe with a 5-hp outboard motor. Remove the thwarts in the canoe, fill it to above the gunnels with lumber and replace the thwarts. Two 18' canoes can be rafted together side-by-side and filled with lumber.

7. Lay out logs for the cabin footprint, then place 4x4s across the logs on 24" centers for the flooring. Build the walls eight feet high using 2x4s on 16"

centers. Build the cabin 12' high at the gable ends and no more than 20' long, as the sawmill can only make a 20' beam.

8. Order materials from the "outside," such as cement for footings, tarpaper and asphalt shingles for the roof, windows, doors and insulation. Stoves and refrigerators also need to be ordered.

The beginnings of a frame cabin

Building chores were never finished when the cabins were built. Each cabin owner needed storage buildings, woodsheds, wood stoves, outhouses, ice houses, docks, power plant sheds, refrigerators and many other additional features. At their own resort, Betsy and Frank built an assortment of outbuildings, including an ice-house, an airplane hanger, a gasoline storage shed and a snow machine storage shed. Once those were completed, they required maintenance and repair. Once again, Betsy and Frank were always available to do the work.

Log Cabins Built by Betsy and Frank

1. Island across from the sand beach on Northern Light Lake. (Karl Kinenzie, Dr. William Ackermann and John Bloomdahl)

2. North side of the island in Trafalger Bay on Northern Light Lake (Art and Virginia Vidich)

3. Lee Island in Saganaga Lake (Don Hayward)

4. Island just before Horsetail Falls on Saganaga Lake (Ed Kohl)

5. Clark's Island—this was the last log cabin built by Frank and Betsy (Noble Clark)

6. Saganagons Lake for Green Forest Resort (Frank Powell)

Frame Cabins Built by Betsy and Frank

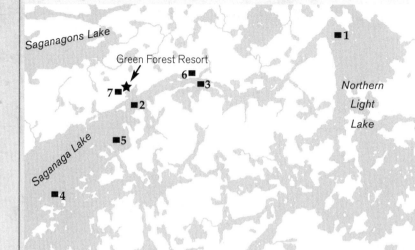

1. South end of island in Trafalgar Bay of Northern Light Lake

2. Landergott Island (Formerly Magnuson who was related to Bally in Grand Marais)

3. Island across from Horsetail Falls on Saganaga Lake (Dr. Braun)

4. Chic Wauk Island in Saganaga Lake for Borderland Lodge

5. Across from Irv Benson's place on Saganaga Lake (The Taylor's)

6. At Clayton's on the north side of Saganaga Lake

7. At Green Forest Resort

Betsy's Cabin

Betsy and Frank in front of her newly-completed cabin

In 1955, Betsy felt it was time to build her own cabin. She had waited until she knew exactly what she was doing. It was a comfortable 16' by 20' cabin where Betsy lived for more than 50 years. Finally, Betsy had built a place of her own! Frank moved in with Betsy then, although Charlotte remained at the resort cooking and cleaning for lake residents until 1970. After leaving the resort, Charlotte remained on Saganaga for a few years more, but eventually left the area. Betsy and Frank were married in 1971; they never had children.

Betsy's pride and joy: her cabin in the winter

Chapter Glossary

Boom:
Logs fastened together end to end used to contain floating logs within.

Cant hook:
A wooden pole with a curved iron hook used to handle and move logs.

Cross-cut saw:
A saw with a very long blade and two handles at the ends to allow two people to use it.

Draw knife:
A blade with perpendicular handles on each end.

Gunnels:
The widened edge at the top of the sides of a canoe.

Scribe:
To make notches in the wood with an ax.

Thwarts:
The crosspieces spreading horizontally across a canoe.

Chapter 8

The Ice Harvest

Just as the summer waters of Saganaga provided a bounty of fish, the winter ice provided a harvest as well—an ice harvest. Beginning in the 1950s Betsy and Frank harvested ice on Saganaga and Saganagons. Ice was used to support the summer fishing business and to provide a small source of income. Fishermen, who were arriving in greater numbers every year, expected to keep their beer cold and their fish fresh for transportation home.

Harvesting the huge ice field outside of Betsy's cabin at Saganaga

Every year, from 1950 to 1965, as the ice was forming on the lake, the fields from which Betsy and Frank would harvest the ice would be planned. The main ice field was just offshore in front of Betsy's cabin on Saganaga. As soon as the snow started falling, Betsy and Frank would begin shoveling and shoveling and shoveling. There were two reasons to shovel: without snow, the ice would form faster (requiring less shoveling in the long run) and snowless ice was necessary when the harvest began.

"You had to shovel a much larger area than you planned to cut," explains Betsy, "and as more snow accumulated, a larger space needed to be shoveled. If you didn't shovel enough, the weight of the snow would force the water onto the ice when the cutting started, flooding the ice field and ruining the ice harvest."

Shoveling continued until sometime between Christmas and New Year's Day, when the ice would be "ready." The ice harvest could occur in any kind of weather, but it was best when it was not snowing. When a 2" test hole augered into the ice showed an ice depth of 12" to 18", the ice harvest could begin.

In one day Betsy and Frank cut 800 to 900 ice cakes, each ice cake measuring 16" on a side. Six hundred of those cakes were used for their own resort, with the rest sold to the Taylors at Merrill Island and to Shady Rest Resort. Betsy and Frank also shoveled ice fields and harvested ice for Jack Powell and several other residents along Saganagons Lake.

Harvesting by Hand

Ice was cut by hand at Saganagons. Frank would cut using an ice saw with a 7' blade, marking a straight line with a piece of lumber.

This worked for a small ice harvest but was not practical when the order called for hundreds of cakes. Using what he had on hand, Frank built an ice-cutting machine from a leftover 36" sawmill blade and powered it with a Clinton engine from an

Frank cutting ice by hand using an ice saw and a piece of lumber on Saganagons

Frank uses the ice-cutting machine made from a 36" sawmill blade and powered with a Clinton engine from an old snow machine. Charlotte shovels the field for the harvest.

old snow machine. Frank would pull the machine across the ice using a piece of angle iron to maintain a straight line from row to row. He would cut the entire field with this machine before he started to break out any ice cakes. When the cutting was finished, Frank would punch out the individual ice cakes with an ice chisel and push them around in the water with a pike pole toward Betsy.

Frank pushing the ice cakes across the open water of the ice field to Betsy for removal

Betsy grabs the 100–150 lb blocks of ice with tongs, hauls them to land and stacks them for moving to the ice house for the summer supply of ice for the resort and its guests

Betsy would grab each cake with her ice tongs, pull it from the water and stack it near shore. In one day she would pull out 800 to 900 cakes, each weighing 100 to 150 pounds.

After the ice was harvested and stacked, it was moved to the icehouses. The ice cakes could remain stacked for some time, but the longer Betsy and Frank waited to move them into the icehouse or transport them to other cabins, the harder the work. They could put eight to ten ice cakes on a sled and pull them uphill

Transporting the ice blocks up the hill, then pushing and pulling them into the icehouse for storage using metal piping

to the icehouse with a powered winch. Frank's favorite engine for this job was the Clinton engine from his snow machine—it apparently performed much better as a stationary motor than on a snow machine.

Ice cakes were packed in snow as they were stacked by hand in the icehouse. When stacking was complete, sawdust was packed on the sides and the top—12" to 18"

Frank sawing frozen blocks of sawdust. Sawdust was the best way to keep ice frozen throughout the spring and summer months, and Frank and Betsy used it to insulate the ice in the icehouses.

of sawdust was packed onto the sides and 24" on top. Frank's icehouse did not have a roof on it. "It didn't need one," he said, "the summer rain would soak into the sawdust and evaporate to preserve the ice."

Ice cakes were transported down Saganaga Lake on sleds in the winter to the other icehouses. Each sled could carry six to eight cakes a trip.

Once on site, the ice cakes were pushed and pulled into the icehouses by hand on runners made of water pipe. Cutting, stacking, transporting and packing ice took all of January. By fall, the icehouses were empty again and ready for a new harvest.

Putting ice onto a snow machine to transport to neighboring resorts and cabins

There was something satisfying about harvesting ice. New ice formed immediately and it seemed as though something valuable had been harvested from the land without any impact. In addition, instead of burning propane for refrigeration, which would happen in later years, all the energy expended to "make ice" was human energy—and Betsy and Frank had an unending supply of that.

Chapter 9

Going for Supplies

Going for supplies was a chore. It could take hours or days, but it needed to be done no matter what the weather, no matter what the priorities of the season at home. Yet going for supplies was also an opportunity to get away, to visit with neighbors along the route, to get news from the outside and to enjoy, step-by-step or stroke-by-stroke, the beauty of this country.

A man or a woman has a lot of time to think when snowshoeing 12 miles across the international boundary and down the lake one way for mail. The mind wanders from worries about chores left undone at home to the color

Frank and Betsy in 1947 heading home with supplies

of the sky at twilight at 22 degrees below zero and finally to the sound of one's own footsteps rhythmically cutting into the silent air. Viewed from above, this scene must be humbling. Imagine one lone figure set against the miles and miles of white, moving slowly and purposefully toward a destination. Viewed from the ground, the scene is inspiring—one lone figure alive and thriving in the wilderness.

In the days before the Gunflint Trail was built, Frank traveled southwest to Winton-Ely, Minnesota or 50 miles north to Kashabowie, Ontario. The destination depended on weather, travel conditions and the price of furs. The furs would be traded for goods that they could not provide for themselves. The quantity of sup-

Carrying supplies required a strong back, healthy feet and a firm resolve. Whether portaging fishing gear, as in these photos of Frank and Betsy, or Frank's supply trips to Ely, they had the needed characteristics.

plies they bought depended on the market price for furs, how much could be carried back and how much room was left in the root cellar at home.

Most impressive among the tasks associated with going for supplies, however, is how many times the supplies are carried before they are at their final destination. Groceries are carried from the market shelf to the cart, from the cart to the car, from the car to the dock, from the dock into the boat, from the boat to the dock at home and from the dock to the cabin. Propane tanks delivered to the landing must be rolled to the dock, lifted into the boat, transported carefully across the lake, wrestled out of the boat onto the dock and then carried uphill to the cabins.

Bill, Frank and Jack Powell and Mary Ottertail taking winter supplies home from Winton-Ely

It is no wonder that Betsy bought only what she needed and saved old and broken things rather than throwing them away—bringing home something new or different required a lot of work and more money, paid as Canadian duty.

In the summer supplies were transported up the Gunflint Trail. When the Gunflint Trail was extended to the waters of Saganaga, lake residents would have their supplies delivered to either the resorts (Chik Wauk or End of the Trail) or later to the public landing. Residents would often pick up each other's

Betsy daringly grabs on to the horns of a bull moose while out on a boat on the lake

deliveries to save an extra trip down the lake as taking the Gunflint Trail was the easiest option, traveling to Grand Marais or the landing took time and energy, and crossing an international boundary to get groceries and mail was a costly and sometimes complicated event.

Traveling to the landing in the summer was easier on the body but took just as much time as traveling in the winter. Outboard motors were unreliable and not

Frank and Betsy by a campfire in the woods

very powerful (usually 3 hp), the boats were heavily loaded with supplies and the winds on the lake could sentence the journey to hours of struggle in each direction. If the engine quit, rowing was the only option—12 miles each way.

In the wintertime, snowshoeing to the landing would take four to six hours, depending on snow and travel conditions. This meant that much of the trip was in the dark. In the years after the war, up until the mid 1950s, Betsy would snowshoe to the landing alone. These trips, no doubt, contributed to the fact that when Betsy was in her 70s she had to have both knees replaced.

Boats and airplanes were essential transportation in and around Saganaga

In the winters after Betsy and Frank returned to the lake after World War II, Frank used his airplane to go for supplies. He would fly to Kashabowie on the Canadian National Railroad line, 50 miles west of Thunder Bay, about once a month. John Harju had an outpost store there which supplied families for hundreds of miles as there was no road yet through this area of Canada. The outpost was a two-and-a-half-story frame building with a basement; the first story was the store and the Harju family lived upstairs.

On a lake as big as Saganaga, there were places where the water flowed all winter.

Frank, Betsy and Frankie; snowshoes, guns, and trapping supplies were fundamental items

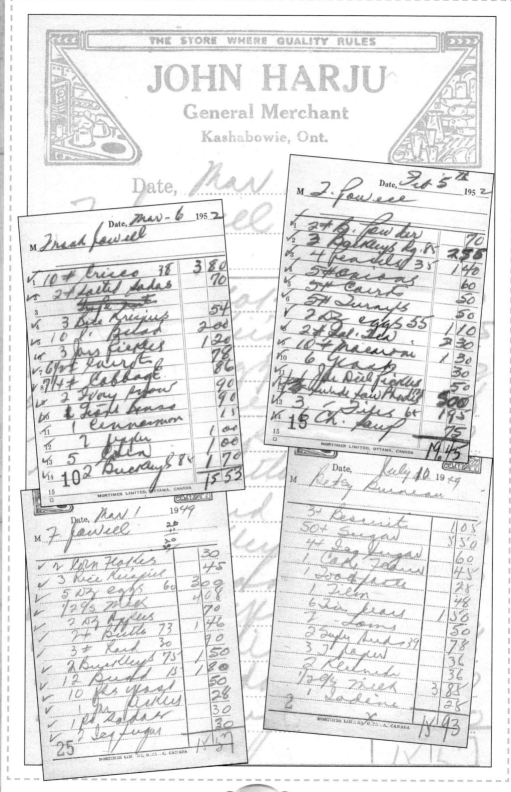

Even with 40" to 60" of ice, in the right spot anyone could fall through the ice. Those "spots" were discovered the hard way and the stories and superstitions about bad ice were handed down from generation to generation.

"Always take the winter portage out of Sag channel; the channel can never be trusted," warned Betsy. "Never go between the rock pile and shore on the way up to Irv's place...and take the North Channel above Brown's Island on the way to camp. The ice is usually good there, in that passage above Brown's Island...but don't walk to shore."

It was a warning given again and again over the years to those who would listen. Most didn't. Those who arrived back at the resort soaking wet and timid were simply added to Betsy's long list of "stupid men."

Old-timers knew that becoming an old-timer was as much a matter of luck as it was of experience. There was always a new slush pocket, a place you might not have been before, or a moment when you are day-dreaming about something else and forget where you are on the ice.

The modified Snow Flea was the safest mode of transportation when the ice was going out for the spring

Canadian Customs

One reason Betsy saved so much—rather than throwing away old junk and buying new—was the expense of paying Canadian duty to bring new items back from the United States to Green Forest Resort.

Bringing supplies to the resort required a declaration of goods with Canadian Customs and the payment of duty. At the beginning of World War II, Canadian customs was still located on Gunflint Lake, near the rail line. After the war, however, a station was opened on Saganaga Lake near Jock's Narrows. Every trip across the lake, from the United States side to the Canadian, required a stop at Customs.

The customs agent would inspect the cargo and then assess and collect the duty. Guests at the resort had to go through Customs as well, declare their goods and pay the duty. In 2004, for example, a supply of propane costing $514 required a payment of $57 in duty.

In 1997, in an effort to save money, the Canadian government closed the Saganaga customs station. Since then, they have required Remote Border Crossing Permits for all lake residents and visitors, and declarations and duty payments are made to the Customs Agent at Pigeon River, 90 miles away from the end of the Gunflint Trail.

Going Through the Ice

Over the years that Betsy and Frank commuted across the lake, and in spite of the warnings that they gave to others, they too fell through the ice. "Same damn place both times," remembered Betsy.

The first time they went through the ice was in April. Betsy and Frank had picked up a load of linoleum for Jack Powell's cabin and other assorted building materials for Frank's brother. They were pulling a sled behind their 1929 Model A Ford heading out into the big lake northeast of Jock's Narrows. It was late in the day and there was no snow on the ice; it should have been an easy trip. They were just about at that spot marked on the modern Fisher maps with a big black star. Frank was day dreaming, no doubt, when it happened. The back wheels of the car collapsed through the ice. Frank dove out of the car to the left and Betsy dove out of the car to the right. But that was it. The car stopped; it was perched with its front wheels on the ice, its back wheels sunk in and the sled still attached and afloat. Betsy was reminded of the fact that this is how and why she learned to swear.

Frank's daydream had turned into a nightmare. But, as always, Frank quickly came up with a plan. He unhitched the sled to save the supplies from going underwater and reached into the icy water to remove the battery from the car (the battery in a Model A was under the seat). It was getting late in the day, so Frank sent Betsy home for equipment and supplies. This was going to take awhile.

Once at home, Betsy packed up the winch, ½" thick rope, an auger capable of drilling a 6" diameter hole, a 6" diameter log, chain, sleeping bags and food. It also seemed like a good idea to bring the dog, Whiskey, figuring he could help pull the sled. Whiskey, however, was not inclined to go too far out beyond Windy Point. Betsy was glad she brought him though. As she trudged silently across the black, snowless surface of Saganaga,

Frank was walking silently toward her in the dark. Without Whiskey alerting her to Frank's presence that night they would have walked right by one another.

Frank and Betsy had built a fire on an island near the car that night, spread pine and balsam boughs on the ground and spent the night in the open. Next morning they started the long, tedious process of pulling the car out of the slush and onto the ice. Frank drilled a hole 6" in diameter in the ice 100' ahead of the car. He forced a log 6" in diameter into the hole. Then, he tied a second pole perpendicular to the first and wrapped it with the rope. Like oxen grinding grain, Frank and Betsy pushed the pole around and around until very slowly the car was out of the ice and slush. It took all day.

The next morning after another night on the island, they moved the car across the ice by rolling the wheels by hand. It took all day to roll it five miles across the lake to the "big channel" on the north side of Brown's Island. There, they rolled it up on shore, removed everything they needed and headed home. Finally, when the ice formed the next fall, Frank installed the battery, started the car and drove it home.

While not related to going through the ice, this photo depicts the many adaptations that had to be made in order to meet the challenges of winter travel

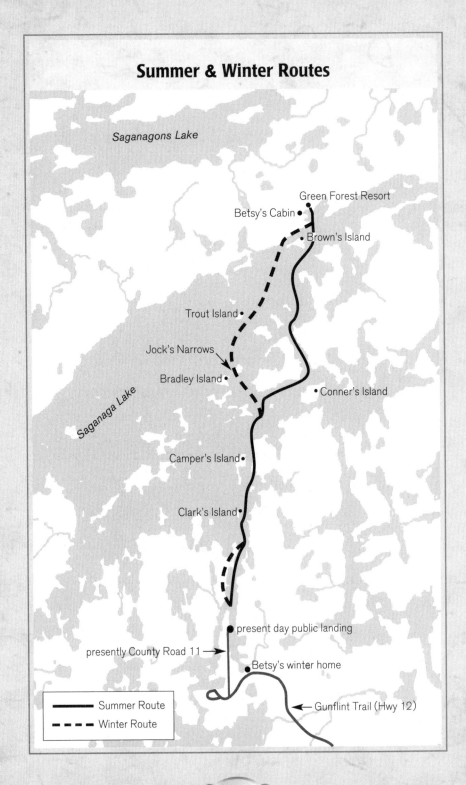

Summer & Winter Routes

Saganagons Lake

Green Forest Resort
Betsy's Cabin
Brown's Island
Trout Island
Jock's Narrows
Bradley Island
Conner's Island

Saganaga Lake

Camper's Island
Clark's Island

present day public landing
presently County Road 11
Betsy's winter home

Gunflint Trail (Hwy 12)

—— Summer Route
- - - Winter Route

Traveling Routes

Over the years the pattern of travel across the lake, influenced by wind and water flow under the ice, was established as "The Winter Route" and "The Summer Route." The winter route avoided spots in the lake where the ice was thin or where snow was likely to accumulate. In the winter, one left the landing on the American side, traveled over the winter portage instead of through the narrows, continued up the channel east of Clark's and Camper's islands, stayed left through Jock's Narrows east of Bradley Island and east of Trout Island toward the north shore, through the channel north of Brown's Island and into the bay at Green Forest Resort.

The summer route was based on finding shelter from the prevailing winds and avoiding shallow passages. In the summer one would travel up the channel east of Camper's Island, then west of Conner's Island, continue north until just south of Brown's Island and on to Windy Point, across the opening to Scandia Bay and home.

Years of traveling these routes provided, at best, a false sense of confidence. Channels and passages known to be free of rocks and reefs for years would change with flood or drought conditions, lake ice and annual changes in water currents. This was unpredictable stuff.

Chapter 10

The End of an Era

In 1975 the Quetico Provincial Park boundary was changed by the Canadian government to include the east end of Saganagons Lake in an effort to adjust the boundary with the natural water limits. Motors were banned and logging, mining and hunting were prohibited on the land where Frank was raised. On top of that, in 1976 Frank had two strokes and a heart attack. The life Betsy and Frank had built together had come to an end.

For years Betsy maintained the resort and took care of Frank. He was unsteady and forgetful, he needed help dressing and bathing, but more distressing than anything else was the fact that Frank Powell would get lost in the woods trying to walk the portage to Saganagons

Betsy and Frank by Betsy's cabin at the resort

Their wedding day, November 10, 1971

Lake. "It was like Frank died," recalled Betsy, "and I died with him."

From 1975 to 1980 Betsy managed the remnants of her life with Frank alone. Helping hands were gone now. There were only two people who remained beside her no matter what, offering their hearts and their home. Mildred and Tumsey Johnson owned Johnson's Grocery Store in Grand Marais and like many others, had been guests at the resort over the years. However, unlike many others, they remained steady and willing companions in the difficult times.

Betsy was a tough outdoorswoman, matching Frank stride for stride

Betsy cared for Frank and ran the resort without his help until September, 1980 when, on the advice of local doctors, Frank was moved to the nursing home in Thunder Bay where he remained until his death in 1988. After more than 40 years of working with Frank to trap for fur and food, harvest timber, saw lumber, build cabins, cut ice and guide fishermen, Betsy had to figure out how to live alone on Saganaga Lake.

Betsy kept the fishing resort open for the fishermen. At 59 years of age, she knew no other way to make a living. Most guests had their own boats now, ice and bait could be purchased from others and permission to cross the international border could be obtained easily from the customs station located on Saganaga. Betsy stopped guiding the fishermen and simply provided cabins for them. She rented out five cabins with beds, linens, propane-powered refrigerators and wood-burning stoves for heat.

Fish were often cleaned on the spot and prepared for lunch

Betsy also stopped hunting, fishing, building and maintaining other people's cabins. She sold the sawmill. It was enough to haul propane, gasoline and wood, to clean and maintain the cabins and do the resort laundry by hand. The resort would be different now . . . it was Betsy's Place.

Fishing resorts, however, cater to men. A few women would sometimes accompany the men, but over the years that Betsy and Frank ran the resort, guests were mostly just men— men who were purposely vacationing away from everything in their lives, including women. When Frank was gone, the number of guests that continued to visit declined. Many had come because of Frank; he was as much of an attraction as the fishing experience.

Frank and his pet rabbit

Hundreds of fishermen had stayed at Green Forest Resort over the years and their names fill Betsy's journals. Only a handful of fishermen continue to visit; primarily fishermen who have decided to cope with the present-day motor limitations on Saganaga. Perhaps they continue to do so because they understand that Betsy's way of life will soon be gone, that there will be no one here who remembers, that this particular bond of relationship with this landscape will be broken, and therefore being a witness is a personal tribute to Betsy and Frank.

The islands of Saganaga Lake from the top of Raven's Ridge

Chapter 11

Betsy's Place

Betsy, in her mid 80s, has survived on Saganaga Lake for more than 20 years without Frank. Although Green Forest Resort has become Betsy's Place, she continues to live without running water, well water, or central heat. At 83 years of age Betsy is still rolling the empty propane tanks (weighing 50 to 80 pounds each) in and out of her boat from the landing and from the cabins—she accepts help with the full ones. She splits and carries her firewood and hauls water from the lake for bathing and drinking. She washes her own laundry and the resort's sheets by hand. It is customary to see one pair of white cotton underwear hanging on her clothesline outside of her cabin like a flag—always there—always proof that Betsy is home and that the rituals of her life remain. She has learned to grow old alone and has done so in a way that has not compromised her independence.

Betsy's cabin and her white underwear "flag"

Betsy's typewriter

A long time ago she had left home to escape the iron rule of her father and found a very different life in another place, one that held a man she grew to love. Through her relationship with Frank she learned to be at ease and productive in this landscape, but in the end she has been left alone, with only her relationship to Saganaga. The cost has been high, but she has made her life "good enough."

In the summer, she still lives in the cabin she built for herself in 1955. There are three general rooms in the cabin. The back room is filled with linens and supplies for the resort, as well as extra clothing. The middle room contains the wood burning stove, a kitchen table that holds the typewriter and a few cabinets for dishes, although they mostly contain old papers and books. The porch is where Betsy spends the majority of her time. Her bed is on the porch and the propane-powered refrigerator is there as well.

When a visitor arrives, Betsy sits on the bed and her guest sits on the one chair by the refrigerator. It is a pleasant place perched on bedrock with a view of Raven's Ridge across the bay to the east.

Outside of the cabin is a small yard with an oak tree brought to the lake by Eve Blankenburg in the 1950s, a maple tree planted by Betsy, an assortment of rocks collected over the

Betsy's haven—her porch

The Rock

Betsy sits outside her cabin in the summer and watches the boats pace back and forth, up and down the lake to the Northern Light portage. "No one ever stops," she comments in amazement, "unless they get in trouble." One such story is instructive:

There is a rock about half a mile from Betsy's dock that is located in the path of motor boats headed up the northeastern coast of Saganaga toward Northern Light Lake. Everyone who travels this route knows about the rock. In some seasons and some years it is exposed and easy to see no matter what the weather, but more often than not it is submerged just inches below the surface, and no matter how well you think you know its location, it can still make you a victim.

So it was a few years ago when some cabin owners from down the lake were hauling a load of supplies and building materials. Betsy heard them hit the rock. It busted through the bow of the boat and the passengers had to work frantically to get to Raven's Rock before they lost the boat and their supplies. In a second boat, they motored slowly across the bay to Betsy's place.

She met them at the dock and they asked if they could borrow one of her boats. "What?" she responded, "with the way YOU drive?"

Betsy's colorful styrofoam cooler garden

years and a garden. The trees stand in contrast to the surrounding boreal forest and the garden stands in defiance of the bedrock that supports it. Betsy's garden is planted in broken styrofoam coolers that border her walkway to the lake. The coolers have been discarded by the fishermen. Betsy has filled them with soil and planted them every year with a variety of flowers and vegetables that she finds or that people bring to her. Every year there are tomatoes and lilies and zucchini and yellow daisies. The color this garden provides along the path to Betsy's cabin is delightful.

The sign welcoming guests to Betsy's Place on Saganaga Lake

In the wilderness, there is no such thing as trash. When something no longer works, it becomes a candidate for recycling into another opportunity. The

Shooting Spiders

Territoriality is a natural part of wilderness living, and Betsy guards her territory. Most creatures are welcome, but red squirrels and neighbors are always suspect visitors. Betsy makes her opinion known with ammunition. She keeps a 22 rifle-with-shot close at hand just in case.

Betsy doesn't like dock spiders. These spiders are gigantic, black and furry. Like predators, they crawl from under the dock to sit and stare at you, as if waiting for you to flee in panic. They have chased many an innocent victim off the dock or out of the outhouse. Familiarity does not lessen their impact as they can unnerve you no matter how many times you have seen them or how harmless they are said to be.

Betsy's dock

When they are on the dock you cannot stomp on them to kill them because as soon as you step on the dock, they hide under it. Betsy's solution is simple: She sits on the shore above the dock and waits for them to emerge. Then she takes aim and blows them off the dock. Simple!

Betsy's winter cabin at Moose Pond Drive

outbuildings that once stored ice and gasoline and airplanes are filled with tools left over from logging operations, old outboard motors and winches, used lumber, empty buckets, thousands of photographs of men with fish, old magazines and romance novels. All of these buildings are securely locked at all times, and, as disorganized as they might appear to the casual observer, Betsy knows where everything is.

Betsy and Frank bought a small piece of property from Art Nunstead on the American side of the lake in 1965. They built a cabin and moved in several outbuildings, buildings that had to be removed from the islands of Saganaga when it became part of the BWCA. This location became Betsy and Frank's winter home in the later years when Frank was ill. Beginning in 1980, Betsy moved to the American side of Saganaga Lake into the cabin that

Chickadee feeding out of Betsy's hand

she and Frank built at the end of County Road 81 to spend the winters. Her winter cabin affords her the convenience of electricity, a telephone and an occasional visitor. In the winter she is busy tending to the wood burning stove, writing letters, crocheting hot pads for her sister, reading historical romances and feeding the chickadees.

One of the many chickadees that feed at Betsy's place

Twice a day Betsy stops to sit on the stone step outside her winter cabin with a plastic drinking cup filled with seeds in one hand and a few seeds in the palm of her other, outstretched hand. The chickadees gather quickly on the branches and the railing; they hover and peck and taunt one other as they compete for Betsy's attention. They land on the fingers of her outstretched hand, look her directly in the eye, pick a seed and fly away...back and forth, back and forth. Soon they are attached to her jacket and her hat, waiting their turn to land in her hand and protecting her from the chickadees who rudely interrupt. Early in the winter, a lone nuthatch would sit close by, too tentative to approach. He eats only what falls to the ground, but by December he will change his mind and eat from her hand.

Chickadees share some qualities with Betsy—they are persistent and industrious birds that do not linger or socialize at the feeders; they simply fly in, take a seed and fly off. They eat very few seeds when offered, preferring to hide them in the bark of the birch trees or in the firewood stacked and drying in the wind. The chickadee birds are preparing for a day when the lady with the seeds doesn't come or winter storms keep them close to home.

Betsy bundled up and driving her boat to get her mail

Betsy can also be observed hauling in her winter supplies from the lake to her cabin, back and forth, a little bit at a time. She carries a couple gallons of water at a time from her dock on the Canadian side of Saganaga to the boat, from the boat to the dock on the American side of Saganaga and from the dock to the winter cabin, until she has collected more than 100 gallons of water for her winter use.

This is what you have to do when there is a lot of work to be done and you are too small or too old to do it any other way . . . back and forth a little bit at a time . . . water and wood for Betsy, sunflower seeds for the chickadees.

Betsy's friends come and go, too, as they help split logs for firewood and visit for awhile before they leave. Only the chickadees stay. They visit every day and they notice when she sleeps too late, pecking at her windows in the morning light. In the winter it is only Betsy and her chickadees.

Betsy meets the mailman nearly every day in the winter. It provides an opportunity to catch up on the gossip and the conditions of the Gunflint Trail. For years the mailman was Donny Brazell, grandson of the motor freight Brazells who had been delivering supplies to Betsy since the 1930s.

Betsy's hands

Some of the hundreds of snowflakes Betsy has crocheted now decorate her window panes

In the winter—as is customary for resort owners—Betsy corresponds with her guests. To mail a letter or package, she buys postage through the mailman who carries the plain white envelope with Betsy's money to the postmaster in Grand Marais, returning it the next day with change.

For 20 years every winter Betsy crocheted more than 300 snowflakes a year to put in the Christmas cards she sent her guests. She made a different snowflake every year. Perhaps you have a white, crocheted snowflake tossed amid the memorabilia of Christmas cards and old letters whose origin is no longer a mystery.

Betsy Powell passed away in Thunder Bay, Ontario, Oct. 21, 2007 at age 86. The summer of 2004 was her last at Saganaga and the Green Forest Resort.

While at the resort, Betsy continued making a life for herself in the place that she loved. She occupied her time reading historical romance novels, studying a catalog of vitamins and dietary supplements, eating chocolate, listening to the Sunday morning polka show on Hibbing radio, selling an occasional fishing license and taking photographs.

She also stayed in contact with the world outside by exchanging letters with former guests, friends, family and people who have dropped by for a visit. Her informal "database" included thousands of addresses tucked neatly into a wooden box held together with duct tape. She typed the letters on a manual typewriter daily.

Betsy Powell

Although Betsy is no longer on her beloved Saganaga, caretakers keep up the Green Forest Resort in her absence. The resort is no longer open for business, but survived the epic forest fires of 2007 and stands to this day as a lasting reminder of Betsy's self-reliant spirit and her lifelong connection to this magnificent lake and the untamed wilderness that surrounds it.

Appendix

Timeline

1901 . . . . .Jack Powell and Mary Ottertail marry

1906 . . . . .Frank born (December 5)

1920 . . . . .Betsy born (November 25)

early 1920s . . . . .Frank goes to flying show; develops love for airplanes

1927 . . . . .Frank and Bill travel to Tower; Frank takes flying lessons
Frank buys his first plane
Gunflint Trail built from Grand Marais to Gunflint Lake

1929 . . . . .Charlotte and Frank marry

1930 . . . . .Gunflint Trail extended to Saganaga Lake

1930s . . . . .Fishermen arrive via Gunflint Trail

1931 . . . . .Frank and Charlotte's first child, Florence, born

1932 . . . . .No open sale of land in Canada; Frank leases 4 acres and
builds Green Forest Resort (3 cabins)

1936 . . . . .Frank and Charlotte's second child, Ruth, born

1935 . . . . .Bill and Dorothy marry

1937 . . . . .Betsy's first summer at Saganaga

1938 . . . . .Betsy graduates from high school; moves to Saganaga

late 1930s . . . . . .Green Forest Resort very successful
Depression hits fur market

1940 . . . . .Frank and Charlotte's third child, Francis, born
Betsy and Frank move to St. Paul to work at Swift & Co.

early 1940s . . . . .Effects of WWII being felt, fishing business wanes

1942 . . . . .Charlotte and children move to St. Paul

1943 . . . . .Frank and Charlotte's fourth child, Frank Jr., born

1945 . . . . .War ends, open sale of land on Saganaga begins

1945/46 . . . . .Betsy and Frank return to Saganaga
Bill and Dorothy move to Scandia Bay and establish own
fishing resort

Timeline

1946 . . . . .Betsy buys sawmill; Frank buys Gypsy Moth
　　　　　　　　　　Frame cabins begin replacing log cabin styles

1940s-1950s . . . .Fishing business picks up after war

1950s . . . . .Betsy and Frank stop trapping

1950-1965 . . . . . .Betsy and Frank harvest ice

1950-1955 . . . . . .Betsy and Frank tear down old resort; build 5 new cabins
　　　　　　　　　　on Saganaga and 3 on Saganagons

1955 . . . . .Betsy builds her cabin
　　　　　　　　　　Frank moves in with Betsy
　　　　　　　　　　Frank stops flying

1958 . . . . .Frank Jr. dies

1960s . . . . .Winter fishing a permanent service of Green Forest Resort

1964 . . . . .Wilderness Bill passed, BWCA created

1965 . . . . .Betsy and Frank buy land from Art Nunstead on
　　　　　　　　　　American side of Saganaga Lake

1970 . . . . .Charlotte leaves Saganaga

1971 . . . . .Betsy and Frank marry

1975 . . . . .Quetico borders changed to include east end of
　　　　　　　　　　Saganagons Lake; motors banned; logging, mining and
　　　　　　　　　　hunting prohibited

1976 . . . . .Frank has two strokes and a heart attack

1975-1980 . . . . . .Betsy manages the resort alone while caring for Frank

1980 . . . . .Frank goes into a nursing home
　　　　　　　　　　Betsy moves to American side of lake for the winters

1988 . . . . .Frank dies

1997 . . . . .Saganaga customs station closed

BRUNEAU FAMILY TREE

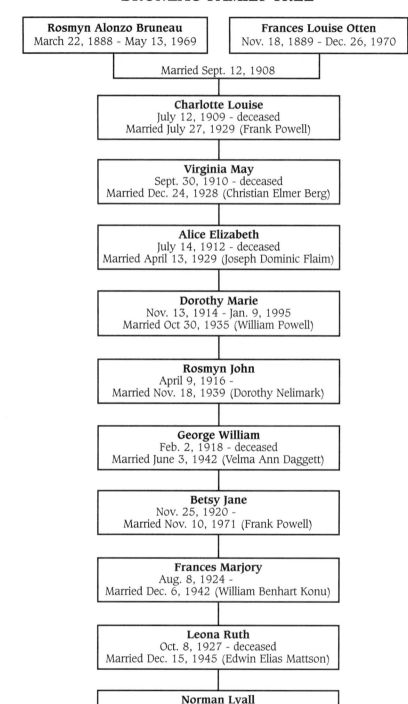

Rosmyn Alonzo Bruneau
March 22, 1888 - May 13, 1969

Frances Louise Otten
Nov. 18, 1889 - Dec. 26, 1970

Married Sept. 12, 1908

Charlotte Louise
July 12, 1909 - deceased
Married July 27, 1929 (Frank Powell)

Virginia May
Sept. 30, 1910 - deceased
Married Dec. 24, 1928 (Christian Elmer Berg)

Alice Elizabeth
July 14, 1912 - deceased
Married April 13, 1929 (Joseph Dominic Flaim)

Dorothy Marie
Nov. 13, 1914 - Jan. 9, 1995
Married Oct 30, 1935 (William Powell)

Rosmyn John
April 9, 1916 -
Married Nov. 18, 1939 (Dorothy Nelimark)

George William
Feb. 2, 1918 - deceased
Married June 3, 1942 (Velma Ann Daggett)

Betsy Jane
Nov. 25, 1920 -
Married Nov. 10, 1971 (Frank Powell)

Frances Marjory
Aug. 8, 1924 -
Married Dec. 6, 1942 (William Benhart Konu)

Leona Ruth
Oct. 8, 1927 - deceased
Married Dec. 15, 1945 (Edwin Elias Mattson)

Norman Lyall
Aug. 8, 1930 - deceased
Married Dec. 15, 1951 (Ann Kathryn Geiger)

POWELL FAMILY TREE

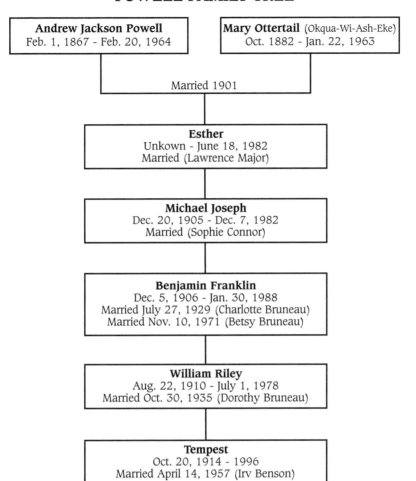

Andrew Jackson Powell Feb. 1, 1867 - Feb. 20, 1964	**Mary Ottertail** (Okqua-Wi-Ash-Eke) Oct. 1882 - Jan. 22, 1963

Married 1901

Esther
Unkown - June 18, 1982
Married (Lawrence Major)

Michael Joseph
Dec. 20, 1905 - Dec. 7, 1982
Married (Sophie Connor)

Benjamin Franklin
Dec. 5, 1906 - Jan. 30, 1988
Married July 27, 1929 (Charlotte Bruneau)
Married Nov. 10, 1971 (Betsy Bruneau)

William Riley
Aug. 22, 1910 - July 1, 1978
Married Oct. 30, 1935 (Dorothy Bruneau)

Tempest
Oct. 20, 1914 - 1996
Married April 14, 1957 (Irv Benson)

FRANK POWELL FAMILY TREE

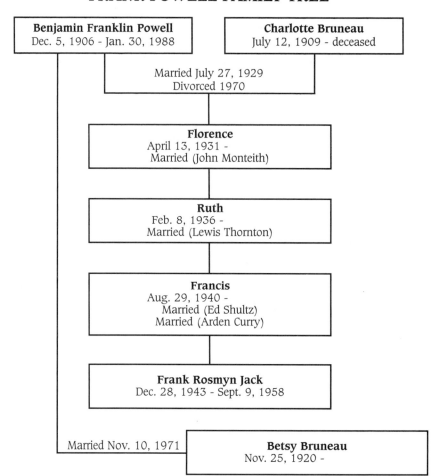

Benjamin Franklin Powell	Charlotte Bruneau
Dec. 5, 1906 - Jan. 30, 1988	July 12, 1909 - deceased

Married July 27, 1929
Divorced 1970

Florence
April 13, 1931 -
Married (John Monteith)

Ruth
Feb. 8, 1936 -
Married (Lewis Thornton)

Francis
Aug. 29, 1940 -
Married (Ed Shultz)
Married (Arden Curry)

Frank Rosmyn Jack
Dec. 28, 1943 - Sept. 9, 1958

Married Nov. 10, 1971

Betsy Bruneau
Nov. 25, 1920 -

NOTES

– The rest of the Powell children eventually settled on Saganaga Lake.

– Esther Powell lived on an island in Saganagons with her husband Lawrence Major until their young daughter died of pneumonia and then they moved to Port Arthur.

– Mike Powell married Sophie Conner and settled in Scandia Bay when he started working in 1930 as a fishing guide for Chic Wauk Lodge at the end of the Gunflint Trail.

– Tempest lived at home off and on until she married Irv Benson in 1957 and settled on Saganaga.

– Jack Powell and Mary Ottertail continued to live at the homestead on Saganagons Lake until 1953 when they moved to a cabin built by Irv and Tempest on Saganaga.

– Bill and Dorothy moved to Grand Marais during the war, then moved to Scandia Bay to start their own fishing business.

Photo Credits and Copyright Holders